Books by Renata Adler

Pitch Dark

Speedboat

Toward a Radical Middle: Fourteen Pieces of Reporting and Criticism

A Year in the Dark

Reckless Disregard: Westmoreland v. CBS et al., Sharon v. Time

GONE

The Last Days of *The New Yorker*

Renata Adler

Simon & Schuster

New York London Sydney Singapore

SIMON & SCHUSTER
Rockefeller Center
1230 Avenue of the Americas
New York, NY 10020

Designed by Jeanette Olender
Manufactured in the United States of America

1 3 5 7 9 10 8 6 4 2

Library of Congress Cataloging-in-Publication Data
Adler, Renata.
Gone : the last days of the New Yorker / Renata Adler.
p. cm.
1. New Yorker (New York, N.Y. : 1925)—History.
2. Periodicals, Publishing of—New York (State)—New York—
History—20th century. 3. Journalism—New York (State)—
New York—Editing—History—20th century.
4. Shawn, William. I. Title.
PN4900.N35 A34 1999
051'.09747'1—dc21 99-049122
ISBN 0-684-80816-1

For Harriet Walden

And in memory of Saul Steinberg

GONE

Preface

As I write this, *The New Yorker* is dead. It still comes out every week, or almost every week. There are the so-called double issues, which resemble, in format, the monthly fashion magazines, and which are "double" not in terms of content but only of duration; they remain on the stands an extra week. Otherwise, not a single defining element of the magazine remains. There have been five editors: Harold Ross, who founded the magazine in 1925; William Shawn, who ran it from 1951 to 1987; Robert Gottlieb, who came in in 1987 and left in 1992; Tina Brown, who took over in 1993 and left in 1998; and David Remnick, who came in in 1998. The magazine was already, at least arguably, declining under Mr. Shawn. This change goes beyond decline. It may be that a magazine has a natural life span and then sputters out. I don't think so. Or it may be that, from the remains of what was once a living enterprise, something else, under Mr. Remnick, or someone else, will grow. Apart perhaps from its logo, that would not be *The New Yorker*. The format, the look, the content, the humor, the level of seriousness; the ambition, at the top; the standards in the middle, the limits beneath which it would not sink; the relationship between editorial and advertising considerations; the balance between prose and pictures; the signature; certain notions of excellence; certain understandings with readers; the institutional memory—these are not qualities that can be set aside and then taken up again.

The New Yorker used, from time to time, to publish the definitive piece on a subject. Readers knew it. Everyone knew it. The facts had been checked; the prose was adequate. The level of attack, the effort devoted to the piece, was likely to be high. Above all, there was a firm sequence: first, the creation of the work itself; then, the publication of the magazine, followed by the reaction of readers; finally, the enlistment of advertisers. An unmistakable sign of vitality in a magazine, as opposed, for example, to even the most sustained buzz, is that it is always a bit ahead of its readers. It cannot chase after them, or pander to what it believes to be their tastes. It cannot follow, or even try to anticipate, fashions and trends. It goes its way, and forms its audiences as it goes. This seems fairly obvious, until one considers that it runs absolutely counter to the mentality of subscription surveys, focus groups, and polls. The strength of *The New Yorker* under its two great editors, Harold Ross and William Shawn, was that it was governed entirely by the curiosity and energy of these editors and of the artists and writers whom they found, without worrying about what readers were going to like, least of all, about what advertisers thought.

Under both these editors, the magazine was financially a huge success. Before *The New Yorker,* there had been, on the one hand, the established literary magazines, *Harper's, The Atlantic Monthly, The American Mercury.* These were supported mainly by reader subscriptions. On the other hand, there were the newer, mass-market general interest publications, *Collier's, The Saturday Evening Post,* which were supported by advertising and which kept the line between advertising and editorial content far from distinct. From time to time, there were also little magazines, like *Dial,* which, important as they might be, were not self-supporting, and did not last long. *The New Yorker* created a readership for a new sort of literary magazine, supported not by subscriptions but by advertisers, whom the editors ignored. It soon swallowed the little magazines as well, by buying up a lot of material that would, and probably should, have appeared in them.

Those little magazines had their patrons. *The New Yorker,* which began, from almost the moment Mr. Shawn left it, for the first time since its earliest years, to lose money, has, in its present owner, a patron now. The yearly losses, which grew over time, coincided, I think, with ever-increasing efforts to anticipate what readers like and to accommodate what advertisers want, in terms of style, layout, tone, even the notorious advertising copy disguised as editorial content, advertorials. There were, it is true, more important factors. Mr. Shawn, and before him, Ross, turned out to have had, in addition to remarkable civility and idiosyncratic but far-ranging interests, a kind of editorial genius, an intensity of focus, on every detail of every issue. As a result, over a period of more than fifty years, the magazine created and met a set of expectations. Its quality might go up or down. But there were certain kinds of pieces that could be published nowhere except in *The New Yorker,* and other kinds of pieces that might be published somewhere but never in *The New Yorker.* That is no longer true. There no longer exists what was once meant by a *New Yorker* piece. When the set of expectations is changed, the pieces themselves are affected. Not just in how they are written and edited but in how they are understood. An audience, for anything in the arts, does not pre-exist. It is part of what is created. When the audience for what had been *The New Yorker* dispersed, while the pollsters were trying to determine the preferences of some imaginary, pre-existing and statistically desirable new readership, there was really no *New Yorker* left. The present owner, S. I. Newhouse, continues to subsidize the magazine, almost as if it were a sort of benefaction—as a Renaissance patron might, or for that matter, as Mr. Newhouse himself supports his art collection. There is at least this difference. Neither the art the Medicis subsidized, nor the paintings on Mr. Newhouse's walls, were expected to make money.

It has been my good fortune to have worked for *The New*

Yorker nearly all my adult life. Other books have come out about the magazine in that period. They do not seem right to me. I began this book, years ago, at what seemed to me the beginning of the end. It now seems to me the end, full stop. Something, under *The New Yorker*'s logo or another, will surely follow. But it takes decades to create an audience and so to engage its trust that a story by Eudora Welty, say, based on a recent assassination in Mississippi; or a book review by Dwight Macdonald of a study of poverty in America; or a tirade by James Baldwin about racial relations; or a series on urban development by Rachel Carson, will all actually acquire not just influence but a crucial element of their meaning from having appeared in a single publication. Many publications, no doubt, will continue to publish valuable pieces. But it is hard to see how the expectations will ever be met under a single logo again.

Chapter One

I first came to *The New Yorker* in the fall of 1963, when I was still a graduate student. I had been recommended by the playwright S. N. Behrman. At my first interview, Leo M. Hofeller, who was in charge of all sorts of practical matters at the magazine, said my timing was unfortunate. The kind of job I appeared to be qualified for had just been given to somebody else. There was still a place in the checking department, but *The New Yorker* did not, at that time, hire women in checking. Just so that they would have my name on file for something, however, Mr. Hofeller handed me a package of twelve stories, unsigned, and asked me to take a few days to write down my opinions of them. I took the stories home.

I loathed them all. In those days, I had hardly ever read *The New Yorker.* We simply did not read much by living authors, at college or in graduate school. I worked very hard on each story, setting forth in great, and I thought utterly convincing, detail what was wrong with it and what made it unpublishable. I brought the stories and my analysis of them to Mr. Hofeller's office and left them with his secretary. Two days later, Mr. Hofeller called and asked me to come back in three months, at which time I would be hired for something. In those three months, all twelve stories ran, virtually unchanged.

When I came back to the magazine, it was unclear what I was to do. I had seen Mr. Shawn by then, and been assigned, temporarily, of course, but nonetheless astonishingly, first E. B. White's empty office and then Katherine White's. Mr. Shawn said he was sending me books, and my job was to see whether "there is anything for us in them." Since the books were already published, there could not possibly be anything for us in them. But I read them, and wrote out little reports. In about three weeks, Mr. Shawn called me to his office. The two first readers of unsolicited manuscripts in fiction were about to be married. It was the magazine's policy to have every unsolicited manuscript in fiction read by at least two people. It would be unfair, Mr. Shawn said, to have the two readers be husband and wife. Would I, he asked, be willing to be one of the two readers when the couple came back from their wedding trip? I would. Could I possibly substitute for both readers while they were away? Yes.

In those days, it was the custom at *The New Yorker* to attach a little form letter to rejected stories, but, if they were better than most, to write in, by hand, "Sorry"; if they were better still, "Sorry, thanks"; and if they were better even than that, "Sorry, thanks, try us again." The stories, two hundred and fifty of them a week, were, with one exception, amazingly bad. That is, they were not what people who ordinarily write would send in. They were not like anything that had ever appeared in *The New Yorker*, or in any other magazine. They were not close. Many of them were obscene and extremely violent. Some included photographs. Since *The New Yorker* did not publish obscene or violent stories, or photographs, there would have been no chance. But I thought, These people have made this effort. You can really only judge a writer by his best work. Maybe these are all just lapses. I wrote "Sorry, thanks, try us again," on all of them. Within a few days, the stories were back. "I have been submitting stories to *The New Yorker* for twenty years," their authors typically wrote, "and for the first time, you seem to understand and like my work." And they would enclose three or four more stories. I had to stop writing the notes. The exception—one story which I thought was really wonderful—was rejected anyway. I anxiously read other magazines for months. I had become fiercely loyal to *The New Yorker* by then. I was certain that some other magazine would publish the story and, by this single stroke, begin to surpass *The New Yorker* in every way. The story did not appear anywhere, and I never saw the author's name again.

At one point, I saw no reason why I had to be at the office, or even in New York, to read the stories. I asked Mr. Shawn whether I might take the stories to Berkeley, California, where I was about to become engaged. "You only become engaged once in your life," Mr. Shawn said. He suggested I take time off, go to California without the stories, and come back at any time. It turned out to be true that I was engaged only once in my life, although, as it also turned out, I did not get married. But I was so touched by Mr. Shawn's generosity that I actually sat down and wrote a piece, about WABC, which was then a pop music station, and continued reading the incoming stories. Mr. Shawn accepted the piece. He said I could write or edit, or both, when I came back. I was gone for just over a week.

In those years, people would often cross a crowded room to tell one how and why they had stopped liking *The New Yorker.* It had become boring, they said, all those endless pieces in the same "*New Yorker* style." The cartoons were no longer funny. Sometimes they were incomprehensible. The whole magazine had lost its sense of humor. The advertising was offensive. It was impossible to take seriously any story or article surrounded by all those ads. In retrospect, it seems clear that those years were, in many ways, a golden age at *The New Yorker.* It was true that humor, in its prose pieces, was dying out; but the cartoons, year after year, by old cartoonists and young, were consistently first rate. The difference was largely a matter of editing. The editors of humor pieces—irritatingly, I thought, called "casuals"—seemed, for various reasons, to reject genuinely funny pieces or to edit the humor out of them. The cartoon editors, Bob Geraghty and then Lee Lorenz, were brilliant and welcoming. The only section of the magazine that could be thought to have a uniform "style" was Talk of the Town, and that was just a conceit, or a convention, to make it appear that Talk was written by a single writer. And it was just silly to imagine that a reader would be distracted from a piece, say, by Edmund Wilson or Donald Barthelme, Muriel Spark or John O'Hara, Harold Rosenberg or Hannah Arendt, by the ads, which were clearly separated along clean, vertical lines—not, as they often are today, slapped horizontally across the page, where they interrupt, in fact literally block, the text. An argument can be made, and I hope to make it, that "graphics," in the modern, designer's sense, is the enemy of prose. To insist, however, that ads distract from text is seriously to underestimate the grip of narrative or argument.

That there was, however, an exasperation with *The New Yorker,* even a bitterness toward it, there could be no doubt. Those readers crossing a crowded room to express their dislike, even though there was an element of possessiveness in their complaints, were not entirely obtuse. Although the magazine was entering one of its best periods, there *were* long, boring stretches. Such times may be inevitable in the history of a weekly publication. There were signs, however, of the onset of more serious problems—some of which were the downside of the magazine's extraordinary virtues. Both the founding editor, Harold Ross, and his successor, William Shawn, were, for example, incorruptible. It was not only that they yielded nothing to advertisers. They were indifferent as well to fame, and to fashions, trends, prizes and even the preferences of readers. Nothing could have been farther from *The New Yorker* spirit than opinion polls or focus groups. The magazine created its own audience and led it, as every truly creative enterprise creates and leads its audience—while kitsch and hack work pander to it. Readers, moreover, could trust the magazine, especially its elaborate and conscientious fact-checking. But the downside of this integrity was becoming this: a moral certitude, an absence of self-doubt—especially in political matters—that became a minor flaw and then a major flaw, which led, I believe, to the eventual dissolution of the magazine. Moral self-infatuation has its own corruptions, after all. With time, almost every other principle of the magazine acquired an ironic echo, a sort of cackling aftermath. What had been a place of originality and integrity began to publish, and defend, instances of false reporting and plagiarism. What had been a place of civility, tact, understatement, became a place of vulgarity, meanness, invasions of privacy. What had been at best a narrative out of *The Tempest* passed through the more deluded episodes of *A Midsummer Night's Dream* and ended in a parody of *King Lear.*

Another set of problems was merely corporate, and common perhaps to all aging, successful institutions governed by a single, strong presence. With time, what has been a staff of talented individuals is overtaken by the forces of bureaucracy. While the talented souls are still devoted to the creative enterprise, the bureaucracy becomes preoccupied almost exclusively with power and with schemes for the succession. Mr. Shawn, it seemed obvious to some of us, never had the slightest intention of naming or making way for a successor. The three editors who were plausible and beloved,

Gardner Botsford, William Whitworth, to a lesser degree John Bennet (none of whom took part in plots for the succession) were driven out, cast as villains, or simply passed over in the periodic charade by which Mr. Shawn attempted to persuade others, and perhaps himself, that he had any intention of permitting the magazine to survive him. Too much of his energy was diverted from the magazine to these futile maneuverings with the staff.

Finally, in the clearest possible manifestation of an ironic echo: the kind of scruple, conscientiousness, and inhibition that were among Mr. Shawn's strongest virtues—his awareness of the power of writing and the harm publication can do—led, of all things, to a mystique and an ethic, unconscious but profound. The ethic of silence. The magazine's ambivalence in precisely the matter of publication was remarkable. There began to be feeling that it was vulgar, perhaps morally wrong to write. Turning in a piece, of course, put Mr. Shawn in the predicament of having to decide whether to publish it. If he rejected it, there had to be one kind of painful conversation. If he accepted it, he was put under the pressure of publishing it. He could, of course, be moved and delighted by a piece of writing, but he had the undeniable ambivalence as well. This hesitation was not only explicit in his conversation. The aversion to personal publicity for editors and writers, the increasing respect for the privacy of subjects were turning into a reluctance to publish at all. It was expressed as well in everything from the often needlessly cumbersome editorial process to the physical structure of the office. Wherever there was space sufficiently wide for people to gather in a corridor for a chat, whole rooms would be built, right in the middle of the corridor, in such a way as to take up what had been the entire gathering space, so that what traffic there was had to pass around them in narrow lanes around the new walls. I have never seen, outside *The New Yorker*'s offices, rooms set up in quite this way. I have never seen, outside *The New Yorker*'s offices, structures that appeared thus to externalize writer's block.

It was not just J. D. Salinger and Joseph Mitchell, two of the most important writers, respectively, in fiction and nonfiction, who fell virtually silent in those years. A common pattern for writers was to come to the magazine after working for years at newspapers, and to be relieved not to have to write for deadlines every day any more, or every few days, or even every few weeks. There was time and space to work on a piece, and get it right. The work would get longer, and the pieces fewer, until there were none, or almost none. If there were any, they appeared in other magazines. Dwight Macdonald used to come in every day to his office across the hall, where he worked on a monthly column—for *Esquire.* Several things contributed to this pattern: "drawing accounts," for example. The ostensible purpose of the drawing account was to free writers from the cycles of being rich, when a piece was completed and paid for, and being poor, in the intervening times. There would be a steady flow of cash to draw upon, as a loan against future work. The result was that writers, with an ever larger debt hanging over them, lost hope and stopped writing for the magazine. Among older writers like Dwight Macdonald, there was a jocular competition to see who might die most in debt to *The New Yorker.* Newcomers, in my time, looked around, saw all the writers who were not writing, and decided not to go on drawing account. This, too, was a mistake. It meant we were, in effect, outsiders with offices.

The solution, in retrospect, was either to have a very forceful disposition, or to proceed like E. J. Kahn. He had an immense drawing account and, apparently, no commitment whatever to silence. He produced innumerable pieces—many of them, in my view, so long and boring that I could not understand, even allowing for the broadness of Mr. Shawn's interests, his publication of them. In retrospect, the answer seems purely practical. Mr. Shawn had to run the pieces, in order to get the debt off the books. This may not have been the real reason. It does seem the most likely. Because another contradiction within the culture of *The New Yorker* was that, in spite of the standards, of courtesy, delicacy, tact, civility, even shyness, set by the editor, coercion, whether in contractual form or embodied in the unhesitant personality—the bully, the provoker of confrontations and thrower of tantrums, but also the implacably self-confident—often prevailed. When Mr. Shawn accepted a piece, he would customarily phone or appear at one's office and say, "I think it will work." He might then add some modest or exorbitant praise. It was unthinkable, in one of these conversations, or ever, to ask how much he was going to pay for it, or when it would run. When the piece was finally scheduled, it was often rescheduled several times, advanced or postponed, or even dropped off the schedule for a time. It was unthinkable to inquire about this—either to Mr. Shawn or to some other writer whose piece had been scheduled in its place. Unthinkable, that is, to most of us. I couldn't help noticing over the years that people who did not abide by these protocols, blunt people, and particularly screamers, got their way. This may have been because of Mr. Shawn's aversion to confrontations. Certainly a source of his power was the determination of non-bullies to protect his delicacy of feeling. There was also an element of mischief in his nature; he may have enjoyed sometimes these encounters with people so utterly unlike him.

In the matter of confrontation, I had hoped to finish this book without addressing either Ved Mehta's *Remembering Mr. Shawn's New Yorker* or Lillian Ross's *Here But Not Here.* I don't intend to discuss them at much length. Everyone is entitled, of course, to his own memory of the magazine. Even if they had not written their books, there was almost no way to write about *The New Yorker* without mentioning Ms. Ross and, to a lesser extent, Mr. Mehta. I have admired work by both writers, and both, though again to a greater extent Ms. Ross, have been friends of mine. I am, come to think of it, one of the few people who have been a guest in both Mr. and Mrs. Shawn's apartment and Ms. Ross's—and for that matter, Mr. Mehta's. Both writers seem truly to have loved Mr. Shawn, or their notion of him. And yet both books seem to me such serious misrepresentations of the man and his magazine that it is hard to imagine, on the basis of either of them, why Mr. Shawn or his *New Yorker* should have mattered to anyone.

In neither book to begin with does Mr. Shawn say anything of even the slightest depth, wit, or interest—on any subject. What both writers quote him at, to the almost comic exclusion of anything else, is praising them. The pattern, the narrative, of Mr. Mehta's book, lies in two recurring anecdotes. In one, Mr. Mehta turns in a piece, with doubts, trepidation, fear that it will be rejected. Mr. Shawn calls and says the piece is wonderful. In another, a piece by Mr. Mehta is attacked, for inaccuracy or unfairness. Mr. Shawn considers these objections and finds the objections unwarranted and the piece as wonderful as ever. Sometimes, these anecdotes, which reflect Mr. Mehta's view of Mr. Shawn's remarkable taste and moral sense, seem to me to reveal, on the contrary, something self-serving and unpleasant. After *The New Yorker* publishes a piece by Mr. Mehta about modern English philosophers, for example, Mr. Shawn and Mr. Mehta consider publishing some letters of objection by those philosophers, in the rarely used Department of Amplification or Department of Correction:

> We spent considerable time going over the letters together, but realized that much of the thinking in them was so loose and the ideas so convoluted and contra-

dictory that printing them would serve only to show the philosophers in an unflattering light.

Refusing to publish letters of objection out of concern for the writers of them seems at best an unexamined paternalism, at worst a form of self-righteous, even mildly Dickensian, villainy. Again and again, Mr. Mehta's evidence for the special qualities of Mr. Shawn consists in anecdotes in which Mr. Shawn simply praises or defends Mr. Mehta's work. It is perfectly understandable that a writer's love for an editor might be based on that editor's approval and support. The difficulty, however, of trying to communicate the value of another human being predominantly in terms of the mirror he holds up to oneself is insurmountable. Out of his own sense, perhaps, of what loyalty to his image of Mr. Shawn would require, Mr. Mehta's accounts of issues and crises having to do more generally with the magazine seem to me quite wrong. In particular, an apparent inability to recognize disagreements in good faith—about unions, for example, or the length of pieces, or even whether a one-part, second-rate piece about Yugoslavia by Doris Lessing might be preferable to a several-part, not really first-rate piece about California by Mr. Mehta—leads him to what are, in my view, wildly inaccurate notions of what occurred and who behaved badly or well. When he turns to his own life, and his personal concerns entirely outside *The New Yorker,* it comes as a relief.

Ms. Ross's book, whose subtitle is *A Love Story,* though it shares and even magnifies the mirror problem, seems to me an astonishing and fierce, unremitting, though apparently inadvertent, attack on Mr. Shawn, his magazine, and virtually everything he stood for and believed. Mr. Mehta's Shawn is something of an unctuous, pious, humorless creep, whose distinction lies in his esteem for Mr. Mehta's work. Ms. Ross's Shawn is an unctuous, pompous, humorless creep, whose greatness is revealed in his feeling for her—and his dislike and disdain for everybody else. This Mr. Shawn is a self-pitying man. He whines and complains. In her prior work, and even in some of her recent Talk of the Town pieces, Ms. Ross's great strength has always been her ear for dialogue. Louis B. Mayer presumably did say, sarcastically (to the producer Arthur Freed), "Knock the mother on the jaw!" and "Throw the little old lady down the stairs!" and, presciently (to the tap-dancer George Murphy, who many years later became United States senator from California), "Hold yourself in readiness!" But not a single quote in *Here But Not Here* has the ring of the authentic. The whinings, in particular, ascribed to Mr. Shawn are unconvincing and are not in his voice. He speaks mainly in thundering, self-pitying banalities and rhetorical questions: " 'Who has blotted me out?' he would ask softly and, it seemed to me, chillingly." "About himself, Bill spoke to me unhistrionically and quietly, with detachment and without self-indulgence. 'Why am I more ghost than man? Who has declared me null and void?' " " 'Who am I? Am I really here?' " And so forth.

Ms. Ross, I believe, not only misunderstood Mr. Shawn. She, again apparently unconsciously, disliked and even despised him. "I'm sure he would be proud to read this story," she says, more than once—a story in which he allegedly betrays the confidences of his children, speaks unkindly, disparagingly, and dismissively about his writers, and behaves clownishly, even preposterously, in public places. On several occasions, on the sidewalk outside the ballet, he allegedly shows her, for example, "how to do an entrechat." He sometimes pounds "his Briggs umbrella (which he carried daily, rain or no rain) on the sidewalk, breaking it." "The breakage would have an instant effect: Both of us would fall into a paroxysm of laughter." These incidents, if true, are not occasions of which even a man less punctillious than Mr. Shawn about his manners, his reticence, and his reserve would be "proud to read." But are they true? There is considerable evidence, both in the book and outside of it, that they are not. Ms. Ross mentions, time and again, that this book is as reliable as her reporting—in which she refuses to interpret or embellish her "facts." But, in large matters and small, she seems to get it wrong. To take just small matters of which one has personal knowledge. As evidence of Mr. Shawn's carefree spirit with her, she says he bought a "Huffy bicycle," and that "among those who borrowed it was Renata Adler." I had never heard of a Huffy bicycle before I read her book. I have never borrowed a bicycle from Mr. Shawn. (I had, not that it matters, a bicycle of my own.) The other three anecdotes in which my name occurs, equally untrue, are equally friendly and innocuous, as are her words regarding nearly every other colleague at the magazine—perhaps to ward off their conflicting testimony, or to placate them for the complaints and disparagements she imputes to Mr. Shawn. In larger matters, however, the "facts" are more seriously unreliable. A short, but by no means minor or untypical, anecdote, for example, about the editing of "Eichmann in Jerusalem":

> One of the most unusual writers Bill decided to corral was the late Hannah Arendt. Bill had a certain taste for her ideas. He read her books, all of which were beyond my field of interest. He told me about her penchant for having cozy evenings at her Riverside Drive apartment, with Susan Sontag, Mary McCarthy, and Jonathan Schell literally sitting at her feet, rapt, adoring, listening to her talk about political philosophy. Hannah Arendt pretending to be *Plato?* It all smacked to me of sanctimonious, narcissistic intellectualism. But I attributed my prejudices to my habitual suspicion of intellectuals in general, and I didn't say anything to Bill about them. . . .
>
> The editing, he told me, would be unusually difficult, because it would be necessary to convert her often cumbersome Germanic sentences into understandable prose. . . . *The New Yorker*'s traditional editing . . . requires enormous concentration, patience, and devotion to detail. It makes every writer sound better, much bet-

ter. I happen to admire and enjoy it. It is so satisfying: clarity, logic, consistency, grammar, syntax, word repeats, devotion to the beauty of the English language—Bill and most of us who wrote for the magazine cared about all this. Every day, over a period of a few weeks, I would drop him off in a taxi—where we held hands, as we did automatically whenever we sat side by side—at Hannah Arendt's apartment on Riverside Drive. Working with her was difficult, he told me, because of her difficulties with the English language. But she started out cooperatively. And he liked seeing her, although he found the apartment she shared with her husband—who taught political science, as she did, at nearby Columbia University—very dark, dismal, uncomfortable, and reeking of Mitteleuropean angst in decor and spirit.

Now, it happens that I knew Hannah Arendt's and Heinrich Blucher's apartment very well. For years, I spent, among other occasions, nearly every New Year's Eve there. It was bright, friendly, and comfortable, and did not appear to reek, in decor or in spirit, of angst of any kind. Ms. Arendt, for that matter, was not teaching at Columbia University, and her husband never taught there. Ms. Arendt had, moreover, no "difficulties with the English language," and none with writing "understandable prose." Indeed, she had written several books, and at least one masterpiece, *The Origins of Totalitarianism,* in English, before she met Mr.

Shawn or had any encounter with *New Yorker* editing. That is presumably why Mr. Shawn chose, in Ms. Ross's word, to corral her. Ms. Arendt was not "pretending to be Plato." She was studying Greek and reading Plato. She could not, at the time, have had "cozy evenings," with Susan Sontag, Mary McCarthy, and Jonathan Schell "literally sitting at her feet, rapt, adoring," or otherwise. Ms. Arendt did not care for Ms. Sontag. Mary McCarthy was in Paris. And Ms. Arendt did not even meet Jonathan Schell until years after "Eichmann in Jerusalem" appeared.

But the anecdote goes on:

> One day, shortly after starting to work with her, Bill emerged from the apartment, his face ashen. He was trembling. I took his hand. It was icy.
>
> "As soon as she met me, she started on a strange rampage of anger and assault," he told me. "Nobody has ever talked to me like that. I don't understand it. She said our editing methods were a disgrace. She said they were 'stupid.' She demanded to know why she should be subjected to questioning. She didn't want to answer any more questions. She didn't want anything in her piece changed. She called me names, horrible names. I don't know what to do." He was shaking.
>
> "Is she demented?" I asked. "Maybe something has pushed her over the edge. Call Susan Sontag."
>
> Bill shook his head, in the negative. . . .

It would have been more remarkable, surely, if Bill shook his head in the positive. Still:

> Three hours later I picked him up. He looked spacey. "She was O.K. Distant and cool, but O.K.," he said. "She answered all my questions. She acted as though nothing had happened. I don't understand it." He had a distant look, one that I had seen in him in previous retreats from violence and terror. I took his hand; again it was icy. "Until I can understand something with the rational side of my mind, I am tormented," he said, apologetically.

It is unclear what previous incidents of "violence and terror" Mr. Shawn had retreated from. None are mentioned in the book. Ms. Arendt was remarkably mild-mannered and soft-spoken. The point, however, is that in addition to making Mr. Shawn look like a simpering fool—surely it was not the first time he faced a distinguished writer who became impatient with the magazine's endless editing, in the form of "queries"—everything about the passage is both superficially and profoundly false: the tone, the diction, the dialogue, the setting, the characterizations, the background, the story, even the logic. Does "word repeats" really belong in the sequence "clarity, logic, consistency, grammar, syntax, . . . devotion to the beauty of the English language"? And, even allowing for the passage of more than thirty years, the attempt at verbatim quotes does not even fall with the limits of plausible paraphrase. It is virtually impossible to say the speeches she recalls for him aloud.

What is more serious is the incomprehension, the denial, with which Ms. Ross dismisses matters so central to Shawn's interests, his experience, his nature and personality—what "smacked to" Ms. Ross, perhaps, "of sanctimonious, narcissistic intellectualism." It is clear throughout the book, sometimes by her own declaration, sometimes otherwise, that Ms. Ross can be ill at ease in matters literary or intellectual. She writes repeatedly about her "naivety" and lack of "sophistication." On the other hand "I was intrigued with *The Sun Also Rises,* the first Hemingway book I ever read, at the age of nine, when I found it hidden under my brother's pillow." It is possible that a "naive" child was reading *The Sun Also Rises* at the age of nine. It is even remotely possible that, as in the lives of role players and fetishists of various kinds, there was really another, secret, Mr. Shawn—that beneath the intensely private, well-educated, sensitive man of broad curiosity, mischievous humor, fine taste, and immense civility, there was this self centered, trite, and buffoonish lout, casting himself always as a victim, who found relief, sometimes in his public entrechats, sometimes in a notional yellow bathing suit, sometimes in a checked cap at the wheel of Ms. Ross's sports car, only in her company.

It is possible, but it does not seem very likely. There is often a tendency among disciples of beloved and revered figures to quarrel over the gospel, the mantle, the true relic and remains. Too much in Ms. Ross's book, however, like the

Hannah Arendt episode, not only rings false, but simply is not so. Ms. Ross says that Mr. Shawn shared three meals a day with her, returned to her apartment nearly every night around eleven, and stayed for hours. Almost everyone who knew him at all well, however, felt free to call him at home at those times. He was there. Ms. Ross says that Mr. Shawn was incapable of visiting his daughter Mary, that she had to come to his apartment to see him. The fact is that Mr. Shawn, along with his entire family, used to go to visit Mary where she was. The inside dopester stuff, in other words, is largely wrong. And there are the things she claims that she simply cannot possibly know. Several times in the book, Ms. Ross refers disparagingly to the many writers who may have said to Mr. Shawn, "I write for you."

> They knew him in a certain way. "I write for *you,*" his writers would say to him. They all said the same words: "I write for *you.*" He would look embarrassed when they said it to him. If someone he didn't think was a wonderful writer said it to him he would look doubly embarrassed. All writers gratefully took what he gave them. He didn't reveal to them what this effort cost him.

Now, it is highly probable that many writers did tell Mr. Shawn, upon occasion, that they wrote for him. Ms. Ross herself says, many times, that she wrote for William Shawn. Although there seems nothing wrong, certainly nothing to invite derision, in that sort of tribute, it is even possible that those words embarrassed Mr. Shawn, and that he said so to Ms. Ross. What takes the subject out of the realm of things Ms. Ross can possibly know, however, is that he "would look embarrassed," or for that matter "doubly embarrassed" when his writers spoke to him in private conversation—or even that "all writers gratefully took what he gave them," or what he did or did not "reveal" to them about what "this effort" (what effort?) cost. He cannot have told her how he looked, still less how he doubly looked, and so on. The whole passage, when one tries to understand it, simply crumbles, which is just as well. Ms. Ross has otherwise portrayed this deeply gracious man as, in his heart, and especially with writers "he didn't think" were "wonderful," as—well, as what?

As hers alone, to begin with. An understandable, even touching idea, allowing for all the distortions of memory and of love. But that does not really fit the case. Some "facts" are, arguably, Ms. Ross's own, to alter or revise at will. She says, for example, that Mr. Shawn and J. D. Salinger were the godfathers, at the christening of her son Erik. In fact there was a single godfather, the film producer Ismail Merchant. But Ms. Ross goes to great lengths, as well, to describe what she believes are the details, not just of her life, or Mr. Shawn's, or their time spent together, but the lives of his wife, his family, his sons. Most of this detail is, superficially, innocuous. A lot of it is wrong. Assuming for a moment, however, that these passages are based on things Mr. Shawn actually told Ms. Ross, over the years, and assuming, as well (what is far less likely, with a highly persistent interviewer like Ms. Ross) that he told her, as she says, without prodding ("I never asked any questions about his past life with Cecille. Whatever he told me . . . he told me of his own volition"; "I respected the facts he told me about himself in exactly the way I have always respected the facts given to me by everybody I have written about as a reporter"), assuming all these assurances on Ms. Ross's part are true, the question is, what is detailed gossip about the members of Mr. Shawn's family—about matters utterly removed from her narrative—doing in Ms. Ross's book?

"He told me everything about his children throughout our years together." Supposing he did (and, obviously, he did not), why is she telling "everything," however trivial, "about his children" to us? The fact is, that she isn't telling it to *us.* She is telling it to *them.* The addressees of a major part of her book are, unmistakably, Mr. Shawn's sons, his wife, to a lesser degree, his writers, and any other competitors for his love, respect, and time. Why else be so knowing about things she cannot know, so open with material that is essentially theirs? What she is telling them is that she knows all about them, that they mattered so little to him that he not only thought of himself as absent when he was with them ("his presence at home was a deception"), he would, unsolicited, violate their confidence. Even if he did (again, the evidence is that he did not), and even if Ms. Ross felt that he "would be proud to read this book" which so radically assaults, at the very least, his dignity and his privacy, there can be no benign explanation for her attempt to breach the privacy of his wife, and of his sons.

In an interview with *The New York Times,* Ms. Ross said she need not concern herself with the book's effect on Mr. Shawn's family, or on other people ("Because it's my life"). She has also said that thinking "what the impact is going to be on other people" is "not what writers do." It is risky to generalize about "what writers do." The notion that they do not consider the consequences of what they write is bizarre. Elsewhere in the book, Ms. Ross repeatedly refers to writers as childlike, or naive, or crazy. She often mentions what she considers the indispensable, "parental" role of editors. "All writers, of course, have needed the one called the 'editor,' who singularly, almost mystically, embodies the many-faceted, unique life force infusing the entire enchilada." An editor might have raised many questions. A checker might have raised many more.

What is striking about this book, however, is not its quality, or reliability as memoir, or its effect upon the Shawn family. It is the element of rage directed, implacably, against Mr. Shawn himself. The source of Ms. Ross's anger seems to lie, not—as is common in the memoirs of other "other women"—in how he treated her, but, more deeply, in what he was. There were places, most places it seems, in his character and sensibility, where she could not follow him. These, his work, his family, his intellectual interests, she addresses scathingly or else denies. Then, in staking her claim to have known him, to have been the only one to know him, she makes a flat-out assault on the reputation and the man. Because even if there was, or had been, some slight element of the Mr. Shawn she depicts—the closet, public Mr. Shawn, as it were, in the private man himself—one thing is certain. This is not the way he chose to present himself to the world. It is a violation not just of what he was, but of how he wanted to appear, and of how he would have permitted any other person to be portrayed in his magazine.

It is also true, of course, that the legendary, saintly, canonical Mr. Shawn cannot be quite accurate, either, had, as well, to be something of a pose. To publish a weekly magazine, perhaps to preside for long over any successful enterprise, inescapably requires, from time to time, capacities for deceit, treachery, cruelty, betrayal, deviousness, convenient lapses of memory, acts of self-justification, faults of every kind. It is probably also true that to be a distinguished editor is, of necessity, to be sincere in different ways with different people, to be, in some sense, not just a two-timing, but a many-timing, man. What is rare, however, is this: to aspire, at least, consistently and over time, to the high road. For many people, the high road is not a factor in their decisions or even in their consciousness. That was remarkable about Mr. Shawn, as an executive. To a unique degree, he tried to stay, in his personal relations and his professional life, on the high road of distinction, honor, kindness, excellence. Not always compatible, those virtues, but he tried. Precisely here, as well, Ms. Ross seems unable to follow or even understand him. More than once, she claims to find similarities between him and Tina Brown. She seems unable to distinguish not only Mr. Shawn's tastes from Ms. Brown's, but his personality and his magazine from hers: "And, surprising as it may seem on the surface, William Shawn and Tina Brown, the current editor, are indeed similar." Ms. Brown "possessed . . . under the usual disguises . . . her own share" of Mr. Shawn's "naivety, insight, and sensitivity," and so on. He was a complicated man. He surely had faults. He may have had lapses of various kinds. He did not deserve this. It is a clear, perhaps ultimate instance of the ironic echo and the cackling aftermath.

Ms. Ross was a major character and influence at *The New Yorker*, in the time of which I write. Through the years, but particularly in the last meetings, when the dismissal of Mr. Shawn had been announced but he had not yet left the magazine, I believe she played an important role. The high road is not a fragile place. Commitments to it do tend to be fragile. After Mr. Shawn, the high road was no longer even a consideration at *The New Yorker*. The time when one is most acutely aware of the high road, and the special standard, in a magazine, as in a man, is just after they are gone.

Chapter Two

For more than thirty years, *The New Yorker* was not only the finest magazine of its time but probably the finest English-language magazine of all time. It was not, like the *Dial,* say, or *Orlando Furioso,* or *Hound & Horn,* a small, subsidized publication which launched a small group of writers and then ceased to exist. It was a flourishing business, and this not entirely because of its editorial vision or financial calculation, but also because of what turned out to be almost miraculous, though largely accidental, features of its design. In retrospect, not least extraordinary was the fact that, in spite of the importance of the visual (in the indispensable cartoons), it turned out, by sheer chance, that the only part of the magazine that was in color was the advertising. Outside, of course, the cover was in color. Inside, everything except the ads was black and white. By a felicity of design, this advertising was always vertical, so that it did not interfere with the flow of editorial prose. What did interfere with that flow was something else. The columns were not really solid and dependable; they narrowed into rivulets of type, which wound their way around cartoons and other illustrations. Readers were somehow able to sustain their concentration all the same.

Readers ordinarily turned, first, to the cartoons, which, quite apart from their excellence, created a bond. There is a particularly strong bond, almost of affection, in an audience that shares a sense of what is funny. Then they turned to the text, fact or fiction. Poetry was rarely a source of great interest. Here the idea that a magazine is, in the end, a person was borne out year after year. For decades, through brilliant issues and dull ones, the magazine was almost utterly indifferent to any tastes or influences apart from Harold Ross's and then Shawn's. There was also the advertising. Critics of the magazine used to say that it was impossible to take seriously even the most serious articles when they were surrounded by so much materialistic text. This was a silly notion, as though it were not possible to read if you are wearing nice clothes, or on a train, with billboards going by. The ads provided, obviously, the magazine's finances. They were even, at best, part of the editorial product, in the sense that their style and occasional humor contributed to the distinct appearance of the whole. The editors were free to reject advertising at will, for its look, its style, its content, its product—no underwear or dating services, then no cigarettes—its resemblance to the *New Yorker*'s typeface. "Advertorials" would have been unthinkable.

Readers renewed their subscriptions, year in and year out, whether *The New Yorker* was in a boring period or not. They removed that brown label when their subscriptions ran out, and renewed. No discounts. No chasing after circulation. No advertising by or for the magazine itself. The writers, artists, cartoonists, editors created an enterprise. The business—that is, the audience and then the advertisers—followed. It ought not to come as a surprise that, in the arts at least, that has to be the sequence: product, consumer, advertiser. In technology, you can have customers, a need, investors before the desired product is invented. Trying to create or adapt a product to a market, in other words, makes sense if the product is dishwashers or military hardware. In cultural matters it does not make sense.

When the magazine was bought from its original owners, an added difficulty was this. Professionals and even amateurs often think what other people do is easy. A lack of curiosity about how somebody else's enterprise actually works, a confidence that you can just stride right in there and do it better, is not uncommon. The people from Condé Nast had reason to think they knew about both art and business. Well-known writers had been supplementing their income for years by writing articles in Condé Nast publications. You might find Norman Mailer, say, on entertaining in Provincetown, or Lillian Hellman on flower arrangement or paté. Occasionally, an editor—in recent times, one editor, Shelley Wanger, at *House & Garden*—would try to elicit and put through a genuine piece of writing. Leo Lerman, many years ago at *Vogue,* had done the same. What became clear, however, was that these magazines were not magazines in the ordinary sense. They were thick advertising pamphlets or brochures, with snippets of writing splashed and scattered through them. And, of course, photographs—which grew out of an advertising medium, fashion, and then became, upon occasion, art. With time, Condé Nast began to splash, and cut, and scatter the work of its photographers as well.

These publications were, financially, hugely successful. They had become admired, and feared. When the Condé Nast people came to *The New Yorker,* they brought in their techniques. Advertised the magazine, and gave discounts on subscriptions. Jacked up the circulation. Interrupted the columns of stories and pieces, with ads cut across the page. Solicited and ran ads in the *New Yorker* typeface, and used many "advertorials." An advertorial is not just a small compromise or concession; it is a form of deceit. The reader's eye is invited to mislead him, so that he will think Journalism, when what he sees is Sales. They used the *New Yorker* logo to endorse products. And even changed its format, so radically and arbitrarily, as to run a crossword puzzle, just to oblige one advertiser of pens. What happened was that the readers who had unquestioningly renewed were soon offended. The advertising for the magazine promised new readers an experience at variance with anything *The New Yorker,* however defined, could possibly deliver. The new, discounted subscriptions, having been achieved at great cost for every single reader, were soon allowed to lapse. These readers, encouraged as they were to chase trends, were not renewers. The magazine, for all its hard-won gossip-worthiness and buzz, was no longer what it had always, inadvertently and against every avowed intention, been—not just a last line of resistance for certain forms and standards but, of all things, *In*. The most fundamental strength of the magazine, its prose and even its cartoons, was finally really overwhelmed by advertising. As in virtually every other Condé Nast publication, the layout made it nearly impossible to find the text.

A magazine in its prime forms an understanding with its readers. *The New Yorker,* at its best, was known to be better than other publications. Even at worst, the understanding was that the magazine would never deceive its readers or appeal to tastes of which they ought to be ashamed. This was certainly not a matter of high intellectual aspiration. The magazine had, from the start, its own form of celebrity journalism. Talk of the Town was an upmarket gossip column, and the Christmas poem, every season, was an ode to the famous of that year. These sections once stood on their own. In the intervening years, Talk meandered to stories based on press releases, then to hectoring political positions. The Christmas poem, which had always been mildly appalling doggerel, ceased to be either hip or funny. But what never happened was that the reader was lured into the magazine and then humiliated for his poor judgment in having bought it. There began to be coarse and prurient pieces and photographs of all kinds.

The difficulty was that work of this sort either alienated

readers or radically redefined them, defined them downwards, in a distinct assault. Not a physical assault, certainly, any more than a flasher in a concert hall can be said physically to have attacked his audience. But not just aesthetic, or metaphorical, either. The first time you go to a concert, and there is a flasher, that is one sort of event. If, on subsequent occasions, there are variants of the flasher, and you become aware that the flasher is part of the program, then it is the notion not just of the concert, but of you as the concertgoer that has changed. You either annul your subscription, or you consent to be described in a new way.

There had been, after all, a time when people raced home to read the latest issue, to be part of the community that read that latest issue. In those years, *The New Yorker* not only supported itself. The magazine indirectly subsidized book publishing. It paid, for example, Truman Capote, throughout the time he was writing *In Cold Blood.* When the book became a best-seller for Random House, and subsequently a movie, *The New Yorker* had no share in those profits. Many books, best-sellers or not, were underwritten by *The New Yorker* in this way. In the early sixties, the writer Edward Jay Epstein went to Mr. Shawn with a proposal from Xerox. The corporation wanted to publish, on demand, from schools and universities, ad hoc compilations of *New Yorker* pieces. The magazine had often run the definitive piece on any given subject, sometimes long after that subject had appeared to be timely or topical. "We don't want a scoop," Mr. Shawn used to say. (He said it to me, for example, when he rejected a piece about popular music and organized crime.) Xerox offered to republish the definitive pieces, in book form, as little ad hoc anthologies put together at a teacher's request. This would be an experiment. Xerox would underwrite the costs and pay royalties to writers. Pieces would be rescued, for current readers and perhaps posterity. Mr. Shawn said no. It would divert his attention from the magazine. At another time, I asked him why *The New Yorker* could not have its own book publishing unit, so that it could share in the profits of books it had, in effect, subsidized. Mr. Shawn said he had had the same idea, many years before, under Ross, but had decided that it would seem unfair to those writers who were not invited to publish books under the *New Yorker* imprint. That seemed simple enough to resolve. Why not make the *New Yorker*'s book publishing branch independent of the magazine? He said that would distract him. It could not be done.

At the same time the magazine supported a lot of book publishing, *The New Yorker* inadvertently killed off what had been the little literary magazines. This was in no sense deliberate. It was, nonetheless, a disaster. Those little periodicals, like *The Dial, Criterion, Locus Solus,* and the others, had not been merely outlets for writing; they had created literary generations, and expired. As surely as there were bars, cafes, various locations where Ernest Hemingway, F. Scott Fitzgerald, T. S. Eliot, Ezra Pound, Jean-Paul Sartre, Simone de Beauvoir could be found until some of them feuded and moved on, there were publications where writers appeared, found each other, and developed before becoming successful in the world. In its earliest days, *The New Yorker* had published only the work of its own band of writers. When Mr. Shawn branched out, *The New Yorker* began to hoover up so much material, and became the focus of so much ambition for writers, that the whole notion of small publications was diminished. When he did buy material from young or unknown writers, then delayed publication for months, even years, the morale and then the work of those writers declined. It is impossible to know how much promising work the magazine obliterated in this way. Probably a lot. It is often said that no matter how adverse the circumstances, real writers write. It is not always true. The ironic echo began to extend to this. The magazine, already ambivalent about publication, was beginning actually to destroy young writers by raising their hopes and delaying too long the publication of their work. Even established writers whose work was too long delayed wrote less and less. And there was always this curious symptom of the magazine's tilt toward silence: when a piece was finally published, or on the verge of publication, there was no element of joy or celebration, no thought of "wait until they see this!" What joy there was appeared only at moments in the process—of writing or editing something to a certain point of near-perfection. Those moments, of course, were rare.

In 1962, *The New Yorker* ran a piece called "Yma Dream," by Thomas Meehan, who had been a fact checker. In the dream, the writer finds himself giving a party for a Peruvian singer, Yma Sumac. His first guest is the actress Ava Gardner. Ms. Sumac asks him to introduce all his guests by their first names. "Ava, Yma," he says. His next guest is the Israeli ambassador, Abba Eban. He finds himself saying, "Abba, Yma; Abba, Ava." In due course, Charlie Chaplin's wife (and Eugene O'Neill's daughter), Oona O'Neill, arrives, and the Italian playwright Ugo Betti; then, the actresses Ona Munson and Ida Lupino, then the Aga Khan. "Ona and Ida," he says, "surely you know Yma and Ava? Ida, Ona—Oona, Abba; Ida, Ona—Ugo; Aga—Yma, Ava, Oona, Ona 'n' Ida, Abba 'n' Ugo." Then, the American novelist Ira Wolfert, the Russian novelist Ilya Ehrenburg, the actresses Eva Gabor and Uta Hagen. By the time he says, "Uta, Yma; Uta, Ava; Uta, Oona; Uta, Ona; Uta, Ida; Uta, Ugo; Uta, Abba; Uta, Ilya; Uta, Ira; Uta, Aga; Uta, Eva," the party is terrible. With vast relief, he finds that his last guest is the Polish pianist Mieczyslaw Horszowski. "Come in, Mieczyslaw!" he says. "I've never been so glad to see anyone in my whole life!"

Several things were remarkable about this story. For anyone who happened to open that week's *New Yorker,* it was a surprise, and it was funny. It has since become a cult classic of sorts—and Mr. Meehan, years later, wrote a hugely successful musical, *Annie.* What was strange was that it would not have been nearly as surprising, or as funny, in any other publication. It belonged in *The New Yorker,* in the particular context of achievements and expectations that formed the magazine at that time. The same was true of the great stories of S. J. Perelman. Of John Updike, Muriel Spark, John O'Hara, Maeve Brennan, John Cheever, J. D. Salinger, Vladimir Nabokov, Donald Barthelme. The stories would appear in anthologies, and lose nothing of their quality. But when stories by these writers appeared in other magazines—*The Saturday Evening Post,* for example, or, later, *Esquire*—the impact and even the nature of the story were not quite the same. The context, *The New Yorker* itself, somehow, mysteriously, became part of the story, and not just an incident in its publishing history. This capacity to affect not just the reception but the actual quality of a piece is one of the defining marks of vitality in a magazine. It is one of the reasons why neither Ross nor Shawn would consider reprinting a piece that had ever appeared in another publication, no matter how obscure. Richard Rovere's great piece on the American Establishment, for example, was published in a small college publication and, in time, became a classic. *The New Yorker* would not re-publish it. By contrast, *The New Yorker,* years later, published a beautiful photograph by Richard Avedon, W. H. Auden in the snow, which had been previously published. It was, beyond a doubt, worthy of being published again. *The New Yorker,* however, had lost one of its defining qualities. It became, in that respect and many others, interchangeable with other magazines.

Well, what else was *The New Yorker,* ever, then? A group of writers and artists, certainly—none of them Dostoyevski, Stendahl, Chekhov, Dickens, Flaubert, Austen, Tolstoy,

Goethe, Melville, James. There were, in those years, no writers of that stature. None of them, however, were Joyce, Proust, Mann, Faulkner, Yeats, Woolf, Waugh, Greene, or Kafka, either. Where were the Modernist immortals? Not in *The New Yorker*'s pages. Nowhere. Not even in the generation-launching little magazines. Edmund Wilson was bringing these writers to the attention of a college audience, but those readers had not yet gone out into the world. By the time the audience was ready, the immortals had already long been published in book form.

With astonishing frequency, the magazine did publish minor masterpieces—John Cheever's "The Swimmer," Shirley Jackson's "The Lottery," Thomas Wolfe's "Only the Dead Know Brooklyn," Irwin Shaw's "Girls in their Summer Dresses," works by John Updike, J. D. Salinger, Vladimir Nabokov, John O'Hara, others—which were, in their own way, generation-defining stories. And cartoons, countless great cartoons and covers—one has only to think of Saul Steinberg, Helen Hokinson, Mary Petty—that became classics as soon as they were published. There was also a lineup of regular columnists, so idiosyncratic and distinguished that when they retired, their métier retired with them: Richard Rovere, Robert Shaplen, Joseph Mitchell, A. J. Liebling, in another sense, St. Clair McKelway.

Mr. Rovere, *The New Yorker*'s Washington correspondent, had almost nothing in common with other writers in the capital. He lived in New York. He wrote with an astuteness and elegance that could be found in no other writer and no other publication. His authority was not conferred by the magazine, however, and it did not survive him. One has only to look at the work of his successors. Elizabeth Drew, for example, had the same institutional title. It was not conferred, either, by the quality of his information. Joe Klein and even Sidney Blumenthal have been, at least arguably, better informed. Robert Shaplen was another writer who could really exist, find the space, and be heard only within *The New Yorker.* Based in Hong Kong, he wrote about the Far East, and particularly Vietnam, as no one else did. When American journalism moved to the left, Shaplen's voice became virtually the only voice that neither told you what to believe nor catered to what you believed already. His stature was such that, throughout the war in Vietnam, not only American journalists but also Vietnamese citizens, civilian and military, consulted him, and communicated through him. He had no successors. Other writers, after A. J. Liebling, have tried Wayward Press columns. In fact, all of media criticism since his time has been more or less based upon it, and proud of its influence. Mr. Liebling's work did not flourish elsewhere. Nor, on the other hand, could *The New Yorker* sustain a Press column without him. When he went, the genre went as well.

Even an occasional ad hoc figure like Xavier Rynne—the pseudonym of a writer who reported, from within, on the Vatican Council of 1966, and then vanished—derived his authority from his appearance in the magazine. Readers could trust this pseudonymous stranger because Mr. Shawn had published him in *The New Yorker.* His authority was conferred by the trust which the magazine had earned—and earns no longer. Nor does any other magazine. It is hard to imagine what readers would make of an Xavier Rynne piece in any publication now.

All these reporters were sources of distinction, and of modest glory. Some of the finest reporting by Rebecca West was published in *The New Yorker.* And yet, just as the fiction writers were not Proust, none of the reporters were quite George Orwell. Art is not a race. It is not really fair or necessary to measure the relative accomplishment of writers; great periods, in all the arts, are relatively short, the intervals between them long. It could be argued that the period of *The New Yorker*'s high distinction was a period, culturally, of the somewhat second-rate. This would by no means detract from the magazine's achievement—might perhaps, on the contrary, enhance it. If those were the decades of the second-rate, the recent period may not rate at all. One of the things, perhaps the signal thing, about *The New Yorker* in its prime, was that it tried to find and save the best of what there was.

Unlike the reporters, fiction writers, or cartoonists, two critics, Edmund Wilson in literature and Harold Rosenberg in art, were established, no matter where their work appeared. For them, *The New Yorker* simply assured a more widespread audience. In their case, too, however, the authority could neither be passed on to others, not to Calvin Tompkins, for instance, or George Steiner, nor survive intact in some other publication. A piece by Mr. Wilson in *The New York Review* or by Mr. Rosenberg in *Commentary* was never as commanding, nor as solid, nor as new, and never quite the same.

At lunch, in my first year in New York, the political scientist Daniel Bell once drew for me, on a paper tablecloth, a family tree of what was then, in the world of letters, the New York political-intellectual community: from the academy (City University of New York, University of Chicago, Hunter, Barnard, Yale, Columbia, The New School) through the publications (*Partisan Review, The Nation, Commentary, The New Leader, Encounter, The New Republic*) and personalities (teachers, writers, editors, political figures; Trotsky through Marcuse, Rahv through Kopkind) to their ideological forebears and descendants. I wish I had studied it and kept it. It was clear, however, that *The New Yorker* was almost completely outside this genealogy. Were there giants, at that time—inside *The New Yorker* or outside it? It seems not. But there was at *The New Yorker,* for reader and contributor alike, identification with an extraordinary enterprise. It was not, certainly, a club or an elite. Publication in the magazine meant only acceptance by a certain sensibility, formed by certain pressures, not least by a sense of limit. The sensibility in turn was formed and altered by the publication of each piece. Harold Rosenberg used to say, when a student hesitated to publish a piece in some not-very-highly-respected periodical, "If you know your destination, and a bus is going there, you don't need to worry about what kind of bus it is, or who else is on the bus." In its prime, *The New Yorker* was not as interchangeable as a bus. It was part of the adventure, even of the destination. Its talent, authority, civility, and charm, even its good-will, were unmistakable. Once any of those elements was compromised, the magazine might continue to publish valuable work, but it was just another magazine. The essence of the enterprise was thrown away.

Chapter Three

Against a wall of one of the narrow gray corridors on the eighteenth floor of *The New Yorker,* there used to be long, ugly shelves, also painted gray, where the daily newspapers were kept in separate cubicles. *The New York Times, The New York Post, The Daily News, The Washington Post,* the New York *Herald Tribune, The World Telegram and Sun, The Journal American*—the last three still existed then, though they were foundering—piled up, were read, became crumpled and disordered, but never seemed to be removed until the shelves were full. Most writers and editors did not arrive at the office until noon. Young writers, and very old writers, as they do at most publications, tended to come in early and work late. Each morning when I came in, I used to head for the cubicle that held *The Daily News.* The *News* horoscope, it seemed to me, though far from sunny, was reliable. The Dick Tracy comic strip was in an inspired phase. Dick Tracy's son Junior had fallen in love with a girl from the moon, called Moon Maid (this was six years before any actual landing on the moon); after a long courtship, they had married. Moon Maid, who always wore a little black dress, had tiny horns with little knobs at the tips. At one point, Junior had found her, in a frenzy of self-doubt, trying to pull off her little horns. He had tried to reassure her, saying that the horns were one of the things about her that he particularly loved. Moon Maid was now pregnant. The question was, would the baby be born with horns, or not?

One morning when I arrived, the *News* was gone. This was not serious. To miss a day of Dick Tracy was a bit like missing an episode of a soap opera. One could catch up. Several days passed. Each morning I came in earlier, and then earlier still, hoping to catch the *News* at the moment of distribution. I suspected the messengers. One or two messengers seemed always to be sitting, either chatting or reading newspapers, on the depressing little brown couch in the last bleak corner of the lounge—which was rapidly being crowded out anyway by the ever-encroaching walls. But no. When the messenger came to put the newspapers in their cubicles, *The Daily News* was not among them. The next day, I arrived before seven. There it was. I took it to my office, read and returned it. The next morning, standing beside the cubicle, was Edmund Wilson. "Have you seen *The Daily News*?" he said, with consternation. "I can't find it anywhere. I've been following Dick Tracy. Wonderful story about Moon Maid. Now I can't find it." It turned out that on days when I couldn't find it, he had it. On days when he couldn't find it, I had it. There must have been a third person, who took it when we didn't have it, but we never knew who that person was.

It was my good fortune to have known Edmund Wilson before I came to *The New Yorker.* I had taken courses with him in graduate school at Harvard, and visited him in Wellfleet and Talcottville. Because the world is in some ways so small and life is so complicated, I even had the wedding ring (inscribed MM EW) with which he married Mary McCarthy, and which Mary McCarthy gave to Bowden Broadwater when they married. Mr. Broadwater, long afterwards, gave it to me. One day Mr. Wilson came to the door of my office and leaned against the frame, in what seemed an uncharacteristic slouch. Then, very solemnly, he drew from his left sleeve a long green silk scarf, from his right a long blue scarf, and then, alternately, from his sleeves, an enormous string of colorful silk scarves. Mr. Wilson was known to be a magician. I had seen him do magic tricks before. For years there was, I thought, in *The New Yorker,* in Mr. Shawn himself, that flicker of the unexpected: the gray, shabby surroundings, the dour presence looming, deadpan, in the doorway. Suddenly, the magician and the scarves.

The course I had taken, in graduate school, with Mr. Wilson was a seminar called Sound in Literature, and had largely to do with onomatopoeia. Tennyson's "The murmuring of innumerable bees in immemorial elms," and Rimbaud's "L'insecte nette gratte la sécheresse"—Mr. Wilson had many examples. He was collecting more of them, with onomatopoeia rather loosely construed. The seminar had room for only twenty people; applicants had to describe their qualifications or special field of interest. One student said he particularly wanted to write about "the sound of corpses floating through literature." "Oh, you mean Ophelia," Mr. Wilson said. "No," the student said, "I want the sound of the sea." The seminar was a revelation. We began to read, not just for meaning, but for cadences.

When Mr. Wilson had a piece going to press at *The New Yorker,* his respect for its checking and editing, while considerable, was clearly less than absolute. In the course of an editing phone call, I noticed, he said "Just a minute," placed the receiver on his desk, and shuffled off for forty minutes. He also had differences with the magazine in small matters, like the respective uses of "that" and "which." In the editing of sentences, I found, there are principles that you get, and take or leave, almost the first time you see them. Mr. Wilson said he thought contractions were unsuitable in published work (no "don't" or "can't"), and that seemed right to me. When Mr. Shawn changed every instance of "exclaimed," "argued"—not to speak of "averred," or "complained," or "snorted," or even "said, sneeringly"—simply to "said," that too seemed right. No unnecessarily ornate or Latinate constructions: nothing ever "transpired," things happened. As has been so frequently pointed out, very little indirection. No

> John crossed the street. The tall, twenty-eight-year-old, Harvard-educated, nuclear physicist from Santa

> Barbara, forgot to look at the art-deco traffic light before he stepped from the oddly deserted curb into the crowded midtown thoroughfare.

In other matters, no publication for which I have ever written was so careful not to attribute to the writer a single word, or a single cut, or a single mark of punctuation, which the writer had not seen and, in some sense, approved. Headlines, for example. *New Yorker* writers wrote, or at least had control over them. Readers might not be aware that headlines, particularly those jarring, punning headlines, which first tabloid newspapers and in due course even literary publications seemed to favor, were written not by the writer of the piece, but by some bureaucrat who considers the writing of headlines his own turf. Or that some editors (after Mr. Shawn's time, even some editors at *The New Yorker*) actually write, without the writer's knowledge or consent, their own thoughts, ideas, or prose into the writer's piece. The process of editing, in fact, can be not only adversarial, but distinctly ugly. There are editors, it is apparently an occupational hazard, who cannot leave a piece, or a line of a piece, intact—eating through a text, leaf and branch, like tent caterpillars, leaving everywhere their mark. The writer tries to put back what he wrote and is told that it is too late. Twice, at publications other than *The New Yorker,* I actually thought of going to the printer, armed with a rifle perhaps, and lying down, rather as political demonstrators used to do, and saying, They shall not print, in my name, this version of a piece.

The police might come, and drag one away, but I don't think there is a published writer who would not sympathize. At least the issue of intrusive and objectionable editing would have been framed.

That said, at its best, *New Yorker* editing in those years was often helpful—in that it called the writer's attention to things he might want, perhaps even ought, to fix or change. When it was not helpful, and when both writer and editor were adamant, there was no coercion—except this: You needn't make the change, but then again, they needn't run the piece. That is coercion, certainly, but compared to publishing, in the writer's name, a piece which he has not approved or authorized, the coercion is benign. A great luxury at *The New Yorker* was fresh galley proofs, almost every day, from the time the editing process began to the day the story or article appeared in print. These galleys consisted of a column per page, until the penultimate proof, the page proof, where the columns were laid out, together with cartoons, drawings, page numbers, as they would appear in the magazine. Then came the final galleys, called the foundry proof, in which only emergency changes—like the correction of errors detected at the last minute—were theoretically allowed. One drawback of this luxury was that it permitted the inclusion, in each day's galleys, of the many queries and suggested revisions of all the editors, copy editors, and checkers who read the piece before it went to press. Hannah Arendt was hardly the only writer to be exasperated by this process. It could be tiresome or silly. It could be just plain bad.

Writers developed their own strategies to deal with it. Bud Trillin, for example, would ask his wife to read the galleys aloud to him—including every mark of punctuation—while he read the text of what he originally wrote. For me, the problem was most acute in fiction. There were not only two cultures, there was an old and growing antagonism between the fiction and non-fiction departments of *The New Yorker,* dating back to the days when the fiction editor, Gus Lobrano, and perhaps another fiction editor, Katherine White, were passed over for the editorship of the magazine in favor of Harold Ross's managing editor, and chosen successor, William Shawn. There was a transitional generation of editors—James Henderson, Rachel MacKenzie, and William Maxwell, himself a highly regarded writer of fiction—and then the fiction department passed to Roger Angell, Katherine White's son, a fine baseball writer, and, until then, the editor of the magazine's rapidly evaporating humor pieces.

Mr. Angell took over his mother's office and had, it seemed, ambitions of taking over the general editorship. He gathered a cadre of younger editors, placed them in offices near his own, and established an overt, superficially jocular state of war with the rest of the magazine. The fiction editors themselves wrote fiction, a conflict of interest which did not exist in other departments. That is, each fiction editor held over all of his colleagues the power to accept or reject not just their writers' stories, but their own. And, of course, for each fiction editor's story that ran, a story by one of his writers did not run. This conflict produced certain anomalies. They could compromise, apparently, on Nobel Prize winners: a lot of Isaac Bashevis Singer, a lot of Jorge Luis Borges. They kept a squash ladder outside their offices, with rankings altered daily. While they cultivated the air of an entirely other order of bland white-collar types, their hierarchy, as described to me by Daniel Menaker, was as follows: "You have to understand, we're a tribe of baboons. The head baboon fucks the next baboon, who fucks the most lowly baboon. The lowest baboon gets to write letters that begin, 'Roger Angell is off covering spring training.' " The fiction department of that time has moved on. Chip McGrath, after a complicated trajectory, is now editor of *The New York Times Book Review.* Daniel Menaker is a writer and an editor at Random House. Roger Angell mostly writes. Bill Buford is chief editor of fiction at the magazine, and things seem considerably more benign and open than they were.

I had no direct dealings with the fiction department. Mr. Shawn edited my stories. In non-fiction, I was edited at various times by Gardner Botsford, Patrick Crow, William Whitworth, Robert Bingham, Rogers Whitaker, and Mr. Shawn. The frequency of galley proofs in fiction, however, began, I realize this only in retrospect, fundamentally to change the way I work. When Mr. Shawn would say, "Now, at the top of galley two, first paragraph, line two," I would say, "Oh, that's all right. I've already changed that paragraph," and hand him another in its stead. Same with the next paragraph, and the next, until, on virtually every day of editing, I was handing in radically revised, or even new, pieces of text—to stay, as it were, one step ahead of the editing. This was, of course, a crazy way to work, but to subject a piece of fiction to the comments, queries, and suggestions of a group, is weirder still. The process became what Freud would call "over-determined," the result of too many disparate motives and agendas to define. In due course, the editing of fiction led to my leaving *The New Yorker*—not, it turned out, for very long. One incident, however, which had a happy outcome, gave me a certain insight into the workings of bureaucracy. I had written a story. The last line was:

> It could be that the sort of sentence one wants right here is the kind that runs, and laughs, and slides, and tips its cap, and stops right on a dime.

It is, of course, possible to dislike this sentence. It is possible to dislike the entire story in which it appears. One thing about the story was, and is, that there was no point to it whatever without that last line. On the last day of editing, Mr. Shawn called me in. Once again, there were all the paragraphs with queries, and I had substituted other paragraphs. "Last galley, last line," Mr. Shawn said. "We have to cut it. They've pointed out that it violates a *New Yorker* rule." The rule was this: no pieces that referred to themselves or to the process by which they were written. The purpose of the rule was to avoid a practice that had become common in journalism. A piece called "Tracking Ol' Blue Eyes at the Front," for example, might describe all the travails and dangers a reporter, in a war zone, encountered in trying to interview Frank Sinatra. The piece might have little information about Sinatra. It might even end with the reporter's never having reached him. This device, the self-referring piece by the resourceful, intrepid, self-referring writer, could not, no matter how amusing it might be, appear in *The New Yorker.* A good rule, but not, I think, infallible. And not really applicable to one sentence, in a piece of fiction. I was in despair. Mr. Shawn told me to think about it. "You'll think of something," he said.

When I returned to my office, the phone rang. It was Stefan Kanfer, a writer who had been my friend since the days when I was the film critic for *The New York Times,* and he for *Time.* I told him the problem. He said, "That's not a problem. Just repeat the line before." I said, "You don't understand. Even if I repeat it, I can't use the second-to-last line as a last line. I need the last line I've got." Stefan said, "I know. *You* don't understand. Keep the last line you have, but use the line just before it, twice." I said, "What good will that do? There's a rule against just this sort of last line." Stefan said, "Trust Uncle Kanfer. I know it will work." And it did work. I repeated the line before last, and kept the last line. The story went right through. The moral, regarding bureaucracy in some cases, I believe is this: give them the illusion that they have won, and in the process caused you pain, and they may be so happy over having virtually destroyed you in a never-ending contest of wills that they may not notice the actual outcome. This is true, however, only in certain cases. In other cases, give the slightest sign of having relented, even in something that does not matter to you, and bureaucrats will be so heartened they will break the back of every sentence and destroy the whole. Either way, it is a quandary and a risk.

Apart from Edmund Wilson, it took me months to get to know writers at the office. Brendan Gill was extremely kind to new people. He introduced us to one another, to other people. He gave me a green leather scrapbook, and spoke of the joy he felt, as a young man, in riffling through a piece in *The New Yorker,* to find his own name at the end. He was, at that time, the magazine's film critic. He said he had had eighteen stories in a row rejected at *The New Yorker.* This was doubtless an exaggeration. At least I hope it was. His two novels, *The Day the Money Stopped* and *The Troubles of One House,* were marvelous. In any event, he had given up on fiction. He eventually arranged friendships between me and Joseph Mitchell, Stanley Edgar Hyman, Muriel Spark, Shirley Hazzard, Howard Moss. He was always arranging things for people. Otherwise, in the halls, in the elevators, the sheer nervousness of being new, together with the institutional shyness, would have prevailed. Our cohort was Gerald Jonas, Henry Cooper, William Wertenbaker, Donna Jones, and, not long after, Jane Kramer, Calvin Trillin, Julie Hayden, and Charlayne Hunter. Ved Mehta overlapped with us, to a degree, but he was already an established writer.

Donna Jones was a receptionist. Jane Kramer came from *The Village Voice,* Bud Trillin from *Time,* Charlayne from the University of Georgia, where she had been one of the two heroic students who integrated the university. Julie Hayden was the daughter of the humorous poet Phyllis Maginley. Gerry, Henry, Bill, and Jane were Talk of the Town reporters in those days. My job was unclear. Mr. Shawn began to send me books to review, unsigned, in the column called Briefly Noted. Norman Podhoretz, the editor of *Commentary,* asked me to review a book of pieces by John Hersey. It included the famous Hiroshima piece, which had taken up an entire issue of *The New Yorker.* I had never read these pieces. They did not seem to me to hold up very well. I wrote an unfriendly review, which *Commentary* published. I began to notice, however, that *The New Yorker* was gradually falling under steady attack from virtually everyone. Like those readers crossing a room to tell one how little they liked the magazine, writers and publications from all over—Norman Mailer, writing about how he ranked against other writers; *Esquire,* preoccupied with what it called the "Red Hot Center"—checked in with attacks on Salinger, Updike, *The New Yorker*'s format, its editing, its staff.

The New York Times Book Review section, in those years, was an exceptionally philistine publication. While the *Times* held to an amazing standard in all its reporting sections, the cultural sections were a different world—of cronyism and power-mongering. The reporting sections, which actually *had* power, were comparatively scrupulous about its exercise. The daily book reviews, in those days, had a sort of serenely self-confident mindlessness. At the *Book Review,* books were assigned to writers who had their own books coming out, and also, quite often, a prior relationship, friendly or hostile, with the writer whose book was under review. I later learned from Lillian Hellman that she herself had twice chosen the reviewer, Mark Schorer, for her own books in the Sunday section. Later still, Ms. Hellman actually asked Christopher Lehmann-Haupt, the chief critic for the daily paper, whether he and his wife Natalie would appoint her godmother to their only child, which they did. When Ms. Hellman died, Chris expressed to me his surprise and disappointment that she had not mentioned the child in her will.

The quality of the editing of the Sunday *Book Review* was such that reviewers expected their pieces to be altered, butchered really, without their consent. No one, at least no writer in his right mind, wanted to antagonize the *Book Review.* To a degree, this was true of the Sunday *Magazine* section as well. Hidden agendas, undeclared conflicts of interest, hack writing and editing—perhaps they are inevitable in an enterprise which wields great power, pays little, and comes out relentlessly, week after week. Things improved somewhat at the *Times Book Review* in response to competition from *The New York Review of Books.*

In my first year at *The New Yorker,* I had not considered any of this. I simply noticed that the *Times Book Review,* which I had always enjoyed and trusted, was in fact full of howler after howler, dreadfulness of every kind. I wrote a fairly long piece, composed largely of quotations from the *Book Review.* The day after I turned it in, Mr. Shawn came to my office. He praised the piece, and said that *The New Yorker* could not run it. He offered to publish one brief section, about the best-seller lists, as Notes & Comment, in Talk of the Town. He ran that section. Within a few weeks, the *Times Book Review* changed the way it compiled and characterized its best-seller lists. I submitted the rest of my piece to *National Review.* I received a note saying that *National Review* accepted the piece for publication. Weeks passed.

In the meantime, Alice Morris, the feature editor of *Harper's Bazaar,* started a book reviewing column, which she offered to me. Alice Morris was a superb editor, with what is, in a critic or an editor—I suppose, in anybody—a great gift, the gift of conveying enthusiasm. She loved, for example, the poems of Theodore Roethke. When he died, his widow sent Ms. Morris a selection of poems from his estate. Ms. Morris chose several, including one which she especially liked and promptly published. It turned out she had published the same poem some months before. I asked Ms. Morris whether I could write under a pseudonym. Weeks earlier, I had asked Mr. Shawn the same question. He had asked me why. I said I thought I could write better, and more easily, if I did not have to consider writing in my name. Mr. Shawn said he knew what I meant, but that it never worked. There were no problems a pseudonym could solve. (Years later, he did let me write under a pseudonym, but that was very near the end of his career.) Ms. Morris had no objection. I became the book reviewer, under the name Elrond, for *Harper's Bazaar.*

When I heard nothing from *National Review,* I assumed they had changed their minds. At *The New Yorker,* at *Commentary,* and at *Harper's Bazaar,* I had received galley proofs before pieces ran. I thought I had better call *National Review* just to check. "Oh, yes," an editor said to me, "your piece is set to run. We are going to run it next week." She invited me to come down and look at the galleys. I went to their offices to look. I was stunned. The piece was not only cut to a fraction of its length; almost everything I had written was changed. Only quotations from the *Times Book Review* remained verbatim, and very few of those. I asked to withdraw the piece. The editor, very polite and sympathetic, said that it was too late. I asked what to do. She said that, customarily in these cases, the writer could write a Letter to the Editor. I asked whether my letter might begin, "In your version of my piece." She said, Certainly. I asked whether I might take off my name and use a pseudonym. She said I could. I asked whether I could use a pseudonym *and* write that Letter to the Editor, under the pseudonym as well. She said, All right. I asked whether I could say, "In your garbled version of my piece." She said that was going too far. Still, the solution seemed reasonable and very decent. The piece, and in due course the letter, appeared in *National Review,* under the name Brett Daniels, which, twenty years later, in another publication, I used again.

One day, Dwight Macdonald stopped by my office and asked what I was working on. I said I couldn't think of anything. I had just written a long piece about *The New York Times Book Review,* which had been rejected. "Show it to me. I'll steal it," he said. I did show it to him, and he did steal it—all the quotations, for example, from the *Book Review.* He also used, without attribution, the section on the best-seller lists, which had run, unsigned of course, as a Notes & Comment. Mr. Macdonald was very jovial and good natured. When his piece came out in *Esquire,* he came by my office to ask me how I liked it. I said I liked it very much, and I noticed that he had even used my piece about the best-seller lists. "Oh, did you write that?" he said. "I had no idea. I thought those Talk pieces were written by the editors." That week, I had lunch with a young writer called Peter Mayer—who, years later, became editor in chief of Penguin, and who now has his own small publishing house, Overlook. I told him my Dwight Macdonald story. He told me he had been asked, by an editor at *Esquire,* to write a piece. He had written it and been paid, he felt, very well. When the piece ran, however, it carried not Peter Mayer's byline, but the editor's. "Well, Dwight did say he would steal it," I said. "Well, I did get paid a lot for my piece," Peter said. It almost seemed fair to us at the time.

Mr. Shawn gave me a novel by Herbert Gold for a full-length review. Edith Oliver, *The New Yorker*'s Off-Broadway theater critic and editor of its Book Notes, said, "You know, Shawn would never admit this, maybe he doesn't even know it, but Gold is the enemy." "The enemy?" I asked. She said, "One of them, anyway." I thought about this. Even though *The New Yorker* was under assault everywhere, Herbert Gold, as far as I knew, had nothing to do with it. I read the novel. I read all his other novels. The books seemed to me not only all fairly awful but all essentially the same book. I wrote a careful but nasty review, my first signed piece in the magazine. Not long afterward, John Updike's novel *The Centaur* was receiving unfavorable reviews. Mr. Shawn brought it to me for a long review. I liked it and praised it. I had been, in other words, "against" the enemy and "for" a major contributor. These, my first two long pieces in *The New Yorker,* seemed to establish a pattern. Unintentionally, over the long haul, but in each instance with absolute conviction, I became, among other things, and with just two exceptions, something of the magazine's unlikely hired gun. The two exceptions were that early piece, in *Commentary,* about John Hersey's book, and a piece, in 1981, in *The New York Review of Books,* about the work of Pauline Kael.

Mr. Shawn sent me, for a Book Note, the first collection of pieces by Donald Barthelme. I said I very much admired Barthelme's work, but I had already reviewed the book in *Harper's Bazaar.* Mr. Shawn said that didn't make any difference, I could review it again for *The New Yorker.* He asked, however, how I had come to review it for *Harper's Bazaar.* I said, I had been for several months their book reviewer. He looked concerned. He said he could not permit that.

"You open any other publication, and you find the same names in all of them," he said. "We don't want the same names in *The New Yorker* as there are everywhere else." I said, luckily then, at *Harper's Bazaar,* I had not used my name. I had used a pseudonym.

"It is not a question of the names," he said. "It is the writing. We don't want the same writing in *The New Yorker* as in every other publication." Alice Morris had by then published a story of mine, under my own name, and I told him that.

"It's different with fiction," he said. He was very nice about it, yet he was very clear. I called Alice Morris and gave up the book column.

In retrospect, after so many years, the conversation reflects several elements of Mr. Shawn's style as boss. He was kind, he was firm, he was probably right. Yet what he said was not quite consistent and not altogether true. The shift from not wanting the same "names" to not wanting the same "writing," even under a pseudonym, for example, to appear in other magazines is a radical shift. The implications are by no means the same. More important, over the years, he most certainly did use the work of writers who appeared "in every other publication"—Joseph Kraft, Joseph Alsop, Anthony Lewis, to name but three—and not always their best work, either.

As for "it's different with fiction," years later, when it was fiction that I wanted to publish elsewhere, he suddenly became very angry. I was appalled and miserable. "Our other writers publish elsewhere," I said. "Bud Trillin has a regular column in *The Nation.*" He became angrier still. "It's different with non-fiction," he said.

Alice Morris, who had become a great friend, called one day and asked whether I would like to do some moonlighting. Among the things she did to supplement her income, she said, was this: She had always written speeches for Elizabeth Arden. Ms. Arden was scheduled to deliver a speech quite soon to the graduating class of a nursing school, and Alice did not have time to write one. Would I be interested? I surely would. What I must do then was to visit Ms. Arden at her office, and find out from her, in general terms, what she wished to say. This was a problem for me. The idea of being interviewed by Elizabeth Arden was, for some reason, far more worrying than my first meeting with Mr. Shawn. "You are not being interviewed," Alice Morris said. "You'll be fine. She just likes to tell you in person what she wants to say." So I went.

In her office, on Fifth Avenue, Ms. Arden actually said, "Let me see your hand, my dear," and held it. I thought she was going to look at my fingernails, but she studied my palm. Ms. Arden told me that her name, at birth, had been Florence Nightingale, and that she would like to speak to these graduating nurses on two subjects. Florence Nightingale, and "nurse power." I wrote a speech, about Florence

Nightingale and nurse power. I enjoyed it enormously. Alice Morris resumed writing Ms. Arden's speeches. I did not get another chance at speechwriting until 1976, when I, perhaps even less probably, wrote the speeches of Peter Rodino, Chairman of the House Judiciary Committee, during the impeachment inquiry.

Donald Barthelme learned, from Alice Morris, that I had written the review of his book in *Harper's Bazaar.* He called and invited me for a drink. By the time we met, he had heard that I had also written the Book Note in *The New Yorker.* We talked for a long time. The art critic Harold Rosenberg was not just a friend but one of the men I most admired in the world. Barthelme had been the editor of a literary periodical in Texas. He had asked Harold Rosenberg to write for him, and Harold had later persuaded him to come to New York. Don had brought me a book. He said I must read it if we were going to be friends. It was Doris Lessing's *The Golden Notebook.* A few days later, he called and asked whether I had read it. I said I had. He asked what I thought of it. I said I thought it was wonderful, even great, but that I didn't think things were as bad as that.

Over the years, Donald Barthelme and I were friends. He came to visit me at my first apartment, a small studio in a brownstone on East Ninety-second Street, and I would visit him in his apartment in a brownstone in the Village. Either he would cook, or we would go out to dinner, but basically what we did was drink, also talk, mainly drink. He liked the work of Kenneth Koch and hated the work of Harold

Brodkey, who hated his work in return. I came to think of Barthelme as the apostle of compression, and Brodkey as the apostle of amplification, and I once said to my friend Lynn Nesbit, "Fiction is going to divide into two schools, the Barthelmes and the Brodkeys." Lynn, who was my agent, also Brodkey's and Barthelme's, said, "There are always more than two kinds of writers." Of course there were. Barthelme would send me his manuscripts. Long afterwards, I sometimes sent him mine. "All right. All right. All right," he once wrote in the margin of what I thought was an elegant repetition.

At three in the morning, in late 1968, I was awakened by the buzzer of my apartment. I lived then in another brownstone, on East Seventy-eighth Street. Don came up the stairs, sat down in the living room, accepted a scotch, and said, "All right. Go ahead and say it. I know it. You think García Márquez is a better writer than I am." I said, Honestly not. I had never read García Márquez. He said, "Come on. You think García Márquez is a better writer than I am, and *A Hundred Years of Solitude* is a better book than I will ever write." I said that I had truly never read García Márquez. After a while he left. Later, when I had gone to Cuba, as film critic of *The New York Times,* several Cubans told me that there was a struggle for the soul of Cuba, between a rigid Soviet orthodoxy and *A Hundred Years of Solitude.* I thought, There is quite an octave between the soul of Cuba and the work of Donald Barthelme. I resolved to read the book. Twice, I tried to read it, and failed at around page one hundred fifty. The third time, I read it through, and could hardly believe how rich a masterpiece it was.

Don was a very active, astute, literary politician. Once he enlisted me to block the appointment of a particular candidate for the editorship of *The New York Times Book Review.* "Why me?" I asked, "what can I do about it?" "You know Max Frankel. You've worked for the *Times,*" he said. "It's your duty." His voice had its note of irony, as his voice always did, in life and in fiction, but he meant it. In the event, I called Diana Trilling, who spoke to Lionel, who did intervene. The rejected candidate never knew what happened; neither did the man, Harvey Shapiro, who actually got the job. He once ran a review extremely critical of the Trillings, and was completely mystified when Diana's letter of protest mentioned, what he thought was a fantasy, that he owed his job to her. Diana herself would have been surprised that she was acting in a sequence set in motion by Donald Barthelme. Another time, Barthelme asked me to send a telegram protesting the candidacy of Gay Talese for president of PEN. This time, I wondered not only, Why me? but also, Why? Don said that, among other things, it would seem to European branches of PEN that the American branch lacked any sense of the stature and dignity of the organization, if it were to have as its head the author of *Thy Neighbor's Wife.* I declined to send a telegram.

In February of 1963, when Hannah Arendt's pieces about Eichmann in Jerusalem began to run in *The New Yorker,* I made an appointment to see Mr. Shawn. I had read other works by Ms. Arendt—her book on the German Jewish hostess Rachel Varnhagen, for example, and her classic *Origins of Totalitarianism.* I thought her pieces on the Eichmann trial were likely to be misunderstood. I can't remember exactly why I thought so, except that her argument that evil is essentially banal seemed to me to reflect rather an aesthetic taste than a moral judgment. In her determination to diminish, as it were, the fascination with evil at the heart of so much western thought and literature—from the Bible, through Faust and John Milton—she seemed contemptuously to dismiss, and deliberately to trivialize evil, in the person of the plodding, boring, catastrophically efficient bureaucrat Eichmann was. At the same time, the accusatory tone of her accounts of collaboration, by the victims, with the Final Solution, seemed to me almost incomprehensible, outside the context of her other writing, about the effects of totalitarianism on everyone, on the very capacity for independent action or even thought. All this I said to Mr. Shawn. I suggested that what *The New Yorker* should do, right after the last piece in the series, was to publish yet another piece by Ms. Arendt, clarifying and amplifying what she meant. An idiotic notion, surely, and also presumptuous on the part of someone who had just begun working at the magazine. Mr. Shawn listened, made polite and calming sounds. I left.

When Ms. Arendt's book appeared, the reaction in most publications was extremely negative. One of the worst pieces was by Judge Musmanno, in *The New York Times Book Review.* He was an old friend of a prosecutor whom Ms. Arendt had portrayed in particularly devastating terms. Musmanno's review was dishonest and foolish. The *Book Review* was, far and away, the most influential publication having to do with books. Mr. Shawn came to my office. The letters column of the *Times Book Review,* he said, was going to matter a lot in how Judge Musmanno's attack on *Eichmann in Jerusalem* was received. If I would write a defense of the book, for inclusion in the *Book Review*'s letters column, he would be pleased to edit it. So I wrote a letter. Mr. Shawn edited it. I sent it off. When the *Review* with the letters column appeared, it was scandalous. Some letters in support of Ms. Arendt were shortened and run as attacking letters. Some attacking letters were run as supporting letters. The book's situation was worse than it had been. Mr. Shawn came again to my office. *The New Yorker,* he said, never defended itself or any of its writers, but this was an exception. If I liked, and if Ms. Arendt herself approved, he would run my letter as a Notes & Comment. I said, fine. Ms. Arendt did approve. The letter ran as a Notes & Comment. Mr. Shawn came once more. Ms. Arendt, he said, would like to invite me to tea.

Thus began my friendship with Hannah Arendt and her husband, Heinrich Blucher. If anyone was, in Lillian Ross's phrase, sitting adoringly at their feet, it was I. Nobody sat at their feet. I admired them beyond measure. Because of my parents, I spoke German. I spent many evenings (including, as I say, New Year's Eves) at their apartment, among a small group of refugees and other friends. I had lunch from time to time with Ms. Arendt. I once received a nice note from her, about a short story. I frequently incurred her and her husband's disapproval. For not completing a doctorate; for going to the *Times*, where I spent fourteen months as movie critic, for work they considered foolish. With Ms. Arendt, Robert Coles, Daniel Patrick Moynihan, and several distinguished astronomers and other scientists, I was, for years, on the editorial board of *The American Scholar*, which was run at the time by Hiram Hayden. At one meeting, at the Century Club, some of us became so animated that all I can remember about it is saying to Robert Coles, in tones of great friendliness, "Do I take it, then, that this is a coup?" And his equally friendly reply, "Yes, it is." The board, at Ms. Arendt's suggestion, subsequently adopted a rule that there was to be no drinking until the business meeting was over.

In the fall of 1965, when Truman Capote's *In Cold Blood* began to run in *The New Yorker*, I thought Mr. Shawn had completely lost his bearings. I made an appointment and went to see him. I said I thought that the pieces violated certain fundamental principles of the magazine. They were lurid, I thought, and sensationalistic. Their structure was of only prurient interest. The "I-want-to-see-blood-all-over-them-walls" speech came, not in actual sequence, but as the climax of the story. The victims, the Clutter family, I thought were props. Crucial elements of the story seemed to me both meaningless and false. I did not believe, for instance, that one of the murderers, in what Capote described as a sort of epiphany, really envisioned a yellow bird. The yellow bird, at the time, was part of a commercial for Northeast Airlines. I thought Capote had simply used this image because the commercial was in his head. Mr. Shawn listened, as he had when I came to him about the Eichmann pieces. He did not appear to agree or disagree, or even to wish I would go away.

Months later, however, when galleys of Talk of the Town, by some veteran *New Yorker* writers, were posted on an office bulletin board, Gerry Jonas, Charlayne Hunter, and I, having read what we thought was a particularly inane Notes & Comment, went to our separate offices to write notes urging Mr. Shawn not to publish it. Mr. Shawn came to each of our offices. He could not permit this, he said. It was all right to criticize pieces after he had published them. When they were in galley, however, it was not all right. He could not have people looking over his shoulder when he made these decisions. We were taken aback. What was the point of criticizing a piece after it appeared, when the whole purpose had been to spare the magazine the embarrassment of having published it? We never again, in his presence, criticized anything in the magazine.

In my nearly thirty years at *The New Yorker,* it seems to me there were approximately seven crises. The first was the reception of the Eichmann pieces. The second was a two-part piece, in the *New York Magazine* section of the *Herald*

Tribune, by Tom Wolfe. Lillian Ross, who admired Tom Wolfe's work, had written a piece for Talk of the Town. The piece, in a parody of Mr. Wolfe's style, was about a playground in Central Park; the main character was a young mother called Pam Muffin. Clay Felker, the editor of *New York Magazine*, was engaged, at the time, to the actress Pamela Tiffin. There was conversation about someone who was "in." These were the days when several publications ran lists of who was In and who was Out. "He's so far in," the conversation went, "he's coming out the other side." Weeks later, Mr. Wolfe's piece "Tiny Mummies: The Land of *The New Yorker*'s Walking Dead" appeared in the *Tribune*. Many members of *The New Yorker* staff, Mr. Shawn in particular, acted, for the first time in my experience, but certainly not for the last, so foolishly as virtually to foreclose any outcome but the one they were trying to ward off. The almost incredibly misguided response became, I believe, characteristic of *The New Yorker* in every crisis after that.

Mr. Shawn, to begin with, tried to prevent publication of the pieces. In a letter to Jock Whitney, owner of the *Herald Tribune*, he implored Mr. Whitney, in the name of Mr. Whitney's honor as a publisher and a gentleman, not to publish the articles, which, in addition to being gleefully unfriendly, were, in fact, largely false and libelous. Anyone who knew anything about Jock Whitney, let alone his failing newspaper, would have realized to what degree this appeal was misdirected. He promptly released the letter to the press. After the pieces ran, *New Yorker* writers sent to the editors of *New York Magazine* some letters that were good, and others so wildly counterproductive as to call into question the writers' feelings about Mr. Shawn. The good letters were not published. Among the letters that ran was one in which E. B. White, intending, apparently, to express his outrage, depicted Tom Wolfe as a man on a great white horse, dragging Mr. Shawn through the dirt—calling to mind, in other words, a shining knight or even St. George. Other writers attempted to attack the pieces by defending themselves.

At the office, Edmund Wilson simply said, "Thought those pieces might be funny. Couldn't read them. Nothing in them."

The story, of Wolfe's piece and *The New Yorker*'s reaction to it, was taken up by other publications. Mr. Wolfe appeared on a lot of talk shows. Meanwhile, Gerald Jonas, having noticed that a lot of the piece was demonstrably false—writers whom Wolfe had described, for example, as never having appeared in *The New Yorker,* turned out not only to have published many pieces in the magazine, but actually to have been staff writers and editors—decided to check everything that Wolfe presented as factual. The piece dissolved, down to the smallest, apparently most knowing detail.

One anecdote, however, was something that had been rumored for years, and that some gossips within *The New Yorker* had believed. The anecdote, which Wolfe repeated several times, was a cornerstone of his story: that Leopold and Loeb, the murderers, in the twenties in Chicago, of a boy named Bobby Franks, had actually intended to kill another schoolboy, William Shawn. "The Cook County Court Record," Wolfe said, "showed" that their intended victim was one "Bill." This fact accounted for certain phobias ascribed to Mr. Shawn and for the way he ran the magazine. Gerry Jonas was not compiling his list of errors just out of intellectual interest. He thought that *The New Yorker*, having already responded so vehemently and ineffectually, could hardly claim it would not dignify the pieces with a response. There seemed no better place, for a funny and well-framed response, than in the magazine's own pages. That seemed right to me. There were certainly *New Yorker* writers bright and funny enough to justify a piece. In case they needed a factual record, Gerry had it. I began to help him with his list. At some point, we looked at each other. One of us said, You don't suppose the Leopold and Loeb story isn't true?

Here we hit an obstacle. When we checked with the Cook County Courthouse, it turned out that the court record of the case had vanished long ago. Members of the boys' families, or their friends or agents, had presumably removed it. That meant that Tom Wolfe didn't have it, or access to it, either. But we couldn't prove it, as long as we didn't have it. Then, I found it. It was in the possession of a lawyer named Elmer Gertz (who later became famous in an unrelated First Amendment case). I flew out to Chicago, and went through the transcripts with him. He already knew the court record well, but we confirmed it. No intended victim other than Bobby Franks. Certainly no "Bill." Just in case my plane crashed on the way home, I sent the facts to New York by telegram.

What followed was a completely unedifying process. Many times, Mr. Shawn called Gerry and me to his office. He told us how much he would like to run a fact sheet, or a response of some other kind. He said that, in this one matter, he must disqualify himself. "They" didn't think it was a good idea. Gerry and I would give up. Mr. Shawn would call us in again, with another idea of what to do and how to do it. They would eventually turn it down again. We accepted this. We assumed Mr. Shawn was wise and that he was right. One afternoon, however, when Mr. Shawn had again described what he thought, in contradiction to what they thought, Gerry said, "Can we confront this 'they'?" I somehow knew that a line had been crossed, irremediably.

Gerry was, and is, a wonderful writer. For many years now, he has been writing the Sunday *Times Book Review*'s column on science fiction. In those days, he could have written anything. He wrote short stories, comic pieces that were truly funny. I now believe that there are some questions you may not ask a magician, and that it is somehow unforgivable to utter, even in the form of a question, any form of "come off it" to someone who, for any reason, is relying on mystification. The "they" was a veil for the "we," which was really "I." Whatever it was, after that meeting in Mr. Shawn's office, every piece of Gerry's, apart from an occasional Talk piece, was rejected by the magazine.

The story dragged on. Mr. Shawn consented to our submitting Gerry's fact sheet to the *Columbia Journalism Review,* which at once accepted it for publication. A short time later, the editors called and said they could not publish it. Clay Felker and Tom Wolfe had put them on notice that, if the fact sheet were published, they would sue. Sue for what? we asked. Everything in dispute was a matter of public record. The *Columbia Journalism Review* itself could check the facts. Did they think they were going to be sued for undoing a libel? They said they had never been put on notice for a libel suit before, that Mr. Felker and Mr. Wolfe had promised to reply to every single allegation, and disprove it. How? we asked. Since these were matters of public record, they could either be disproved at once or not at all. Be that as it may, the *Columbia Journalism Review* must delay the piece, at least until their next issue. They were a quarterly. Sure enough, Felker and Wolfe never answered. The *Journalism Review* (not, it must be said, in its finest or most professional hour) published the piece in its next issue, four months later. By then, not even we cared.

A short time later, Dwight Macdonald decided to write about the New Journalism in *The New York Review of Books.* He wanted the list. Gerry gave it to him. He wanted to discuss its implications. We talked a long time. At the last minute, Dwight called us in. *The New York Review* had now been put on notice: If they disputed the "fact" that the "Cook County Court Record showed" that Mr. Shawn was the intended victim of Leopold and Loeb, and that this victim was identified in the record as "Bill," Clay Felker, and Tom Wolfe, and *New York Magazine* itself, would sue.

They still think, we said, that just because they don't have access to the Cook County Court Record, we don't have it, either.

In the end, Dwight and *The New York Review* were brave. After calling in a lawyer, Tony Sifton, now a friend and a federal judge, to interview us about our facts, and our motives, they ran the piece—just, upon legal advice, attributing, in a footnote, to Gerry and me the sentences about what the court record showed, or did not show.

In 1967, *McCall's*, which was looking for young writers, asked me under what circumstances I would write a piece. I said it would have to be something I could not do for *The New Yorker*, and something as far away as possible from New York. They called and suggested a piece about anti-Semitism in a small town in New Jersey. I said that did not sound to me like something far away, or something I could not do for *The New Yorker*, or something I would want to do at all. They asked what I had in mind. I said, Brasília or Vietnam. They said, All right. *McCall's* would send me to Vietnam—as long as I wrote a piece that was neither military nor political. That sounded ideal to me. They suggested I interview pilots who had bombed a village, and then the villagers who had been bombed. I said that didn't sound so good, that it had the drawback of being both military and political. They agreed. "When you get there," they said, "you'll think of something." I asked Mr. Shawn for permission. He gave it. *McCall's* sent me off.

There are many ways, in the contemporary world, in which people who have never met meet, appraise, and identify one another. Accents, clothes, how much they spend, airline class in which they travel, people whom they know, universities they have attended, things more subtle and ineffable. Nothing, for Americans at least, seems more immediate than institutional affiliation, the place where they work, and in what capacity. Among jobs, in those days, there was no qualification for meeting people that seemed, everywhere, less subject to question than working for a respected newspaper or magazine. It has been my experience as well that, if one were to go to an expert in almost any field and say that one's life depended on finding out whatever he could tell, about his field or anything else, within two hours, some people would reply, "What do you mean? It has taken me a lifetime to learn what I know, and I don't see how you can presume to ask this of me," while others would settle right down and tell you what they can. Robert Shaplen, *The New Yorker*'s reporter on the Far East, and in many ways one of the finest reporters of his time, helped me, helped everybody. I met Paul Hare, Frank Wisner, Richard Holbrooke, Daniel Ellsberg, Ward Just, Tom Buckley, Jurate Katsikas, Horst Fass, and Anthony Lukas, in Vietnam. All of them went on to lives of some distinction. I wanted to write about a young man called Frank Scotton, who had already become a legend, not quite of the stature of John Paul Vann, for the life he had led among the Vietnamese. "Don't write about him," Barry Zorthian, director of JUSPAO, the U.S. military information office in Saigon, said to me. "If you praise him, you'll only hurt his career. In fact, we're going to deny you access to him." At Bob Shaplen's suggestion, I spent my time instead in the village of Ben Tre, where I followed a Vietnamese province chief and his young American adviser, Paul Hare, for ten days.

On the way back, I went by way of Phnom Penh, Hong Kong, New Delhi, Teheran, Cairo, Tel Aviv. I didn't spend time anywhere except Cambodia, and only two days there. Then I got to the Middle East. I happened upon the Six Day War, and wrote a *New Yorker* piece about it. I wrote my Vietnam piece for *McCall's.* My agreement with *McCall's* had been that, if they liked my piece, they would publish it. If not, they would pay me their kill rate. Two days after I turned the piece in, I had a phone call. They had liked my piece very much, the editor said, and they would understand perfectly if I said no to their suggestion. They would like to cut the piece, and rewrite it in their own way. I did say thank you, no. They were very nice about it. They paid the kill rate without another word.

A month later, *The New York Times* offered me a job as a daily book reviewer. I didn't take it. One kind of reporting that I could not do, I had found, at *The New Yorker,* was Profiles, or any reporting that did not unfold in time. I seemed able to report only on events that occurred in real time, conferences, marches, wars, following a province chief and his adviser. The structure was simple. And then, and then, and then. I had written book reviews, of course, and other essays, but books under review do not unfold in time. It seemed one was never properly finished working on them. I also felt that, if you are a critic, and it seems to you that your field of interest is going through a bleak period, you may well be right, but you ought to make way for someone who thinks the period is fine. I thought books, at that time, were in a bleak period. A few months later, the *Times* offered me its movie column. Movies unfold in time. They seemed to be thriving. I went to see Mr. Shawn and told him about the offer. I said what he already knew, that I seemed to be writing less and less. I wondered whether, if I took the job for a while, I would at least acquire the habit of writing every day. He said he understood what I meant, "But I'm certainly not going to advise you to go to the *Times*." He said that, if I was really going only for a while I could keep my office at *The New Yorker*. I had acquired a drawing account, at the time, $150 a month. He said I could keep that, too.

So I went to the *Times*. I had told Arthur Gelb, my boss there, that I wasn't going to do it forever—also that I was afraid, since I always put things off, of missing deadlines. He said I wouldn't miss them, because writers at newspapers never do, and in fact I didn't.

Arthur Gelb had, in his own way, what I had begun to realize was one of Mr. Shawn's great strengths as an editor: the capacity to inspire writers to work. Each man was so extraordinary that one really did not want to disappoint him. But while *The New Yorker,* in spite of its ban on indirection in prose, was a virtual culture of indirection, the newspaper was necessarily direct.

Bosley Crowther had been the *Times* film critic for twenty-seven years. The *Times* wanted to make it clear that they had brought in someone new. I was asked to write more frequently than Mr. Crowther had done. I did get the habit of writing daily. One advantage of being published almost every day is this: The only way to overcome the mortifications of yesterday's piece is to write a better piece for tomorrow. That motive is a wonderful deterrent to writer's block—and one that *The New Yorker* was utterly unable to provide. There were just too many writers, too many pieces. The publication of a single piece became such an *event* in a writer's life, with months, perhaps years, until the possibility of redemption in the next piece, that writers, with even the slightest streak of perfectionism, polished and polished, and, often, wrecked good pieces by overpolishing them. Then they gave up. The ironic cackle. More silence at the magazine.

After a few months, Harold Rosenberg asked me why, with so many people already crossing over into pop culture, I was reviewing movies. My brother, and then Mr. Shawn, asked whether I was ever really going to quit. When I did quit, fourteen months later, and returned to *The New Yorker,* Mr. Shawn was in a rage. Nowhere in its piece announcing my resignation, he said, had the *Times* mentioned that I was going back to *The New Yorker.* Moreover, although I had gone, as the *Times* film critic, to Cuba, and although he had expressed interest in a long piece on Cuba if I would write one, Mrs. James Reston had called him to suggest that her son write a piece about Cuba for *The New Yorker.* Mr. Shawn told her that he had assigned such a piece to me. Mrs. Reston pointed out that I had been writing about Cuba for the *Times.* Mr. Shawn now wanted to know whether I considered myself a *Times* writer or a *New Yorker* writer. Since I had just come back, this seemed an odd time to ask such a question. Mr. Shawn cut my drawing account, from the $150 a month, to $75. As I sat around, thinking that Mr. Shawn had become so cross not when I left for another publication but when I returned from it, a visa for Biafra, for which I had applied well before going to the *Times,* came through. Mr. Shawn said it might be dangerous, and that there were other reasons not to go. Then he approved the trip. I was glad. Whatever the offense had been, I wanted to atone for it. If a trip to Biafra would help, that was fine. I did go. I wrote a piece. Mr. Shawn published it. Thereafter, he always called me by my first name.

Chapter Four

One evening in 1977, Jonathan Schell called me at my house in Newtown, Connecticut. I was a student at Yale Law School. I had gone to law school, in part because, after the events of the early seventies, I believed an American journalist ought to know the law, as a native, perhaps, knows the forest he passes through. I had also planned to go to law school right after college, and changed my mind at the last minute. Most of all, I had gone to get away from *The New Yorker* and its recurring, in some ways constant, succession crises. I felt my side was losing. For years, Hendrik Hertzberg, Lee Lorenz, Bill Whitworth, and I had been talking about the future of the magazine. Over drinks one evening at the Harvard Club, Rick Hertzberg and I agreed that, down the road, Bill Whitworth would be the ideal editor for *The New Yorker.* He was bright. He was kind. He could edit and write. He was loved. He had been a fine reporter, in the tradition of Joseph Mitchell. He had once come to Ms. Ross's office to discuss reporting, and asked to take notes on what she said. Ms. Ross counted this among incidents to be held against him. It seemed clear he was not going to make it. One evening, Bill Whitworth, Jane Kramer, and I had gone to see Gardner Botsford at his house in Turtle Bay—to ask him to consider becoming Shawn's successor. Gardner was a lovely man, and a superb editor. At the rare times when Mr. Shawn was absent, either sick or on vacation, Gardner ran the magazine. He seemed the obvious choice, Shawn's own designate really. Gardner could not be persuaded. He had no interest in it.

I had grown uncomfortable at the magazine. Wallace Shawn was now one of my closest friends. Although I knew Wallace would in no sense agree with me, I was becoming offended on his behalf. I had in my mind, by now, what I thought of as an iconography or theology of *The New Yorker.* Mr. Shawn was the father; Lillian Ross, the mother. The son was Jonathan Schell; the spirit was J. D. Salinger. This family, it seemed to me, was ferociously judgmental. Not all questions are moral questions. I felt that every view held by the three and the absent spirit was being treated as if it were the only moral certainty. The gravest sin was selling out—which could mean anything from having a life in the world outside the magazine, to becoming famous, publishing elsewhere, or disagreeing with the family on any matter whatsoever. Silence and anonymity were virtues. The sign of Salinger's moral stature was held to be his silence. While there was something to this, in an age that wildly overvalued publicity, there was something mindlessly dogmatic and coercive in it, too. After the christening of Lillian's son Erik,

Salinger had invited me for a short visit to his house in the country. He said that the reason he chose not to publish the material he had been working on was to spare Mr. Shawn the burden of having to read, and to decide whether to publish, Salinger writing about sex. This went too far. The writer who originated, and was the most extreme example of, a recoil from publication and publicity had become something of a prisoner of his sympathy for the editor who had become, yet again, a source of disinclination to publish. A doctrinal circle of pure inhibition seemed to have closed.

But worst, in my view, was the position in the matter of the son. Mr. Shawn, after all, did have a son—two sons, in fact. One, Allen, was a highly talented composer. The other, Wallace, was a writer, and brilliant in many other ways. Mr. Shawn claimed he could not hire Wallace because of a No Nepotism rule. But there seemed, except in the case of Wally, to be no such rule. Ring Lardner had been one of the earliest, most famous writers for the magazine. Now there was Susan Lardner. In due course, there would be James Lardner. Long after Woolcott Gibbs, there was Anthony Gibbs. Roger Angell, of course, was the son of Katherine White and the stepson of E. B. White. In time, not only John Updike's son, but also his mother; Donald Barthelme's brother, for that matter, one of my own brothers, all wrote for the magazine. Certainly, for writers, there was no No Nepotism rule. There was none for the editors. Mr. Shawn, meanwhile, had hired Wally's friend Jacob Brackman, and Wally's girlfriend, Kennedy Fraser. These writers were talented. There was every reason to hire them. There simply seemed to me no justification for leaving Wally out. It also seemed to me an act of nearly filicidal aggression, to hire, and then choose as his successor, Wallace's best friend (and school, high school, and college roommate), Jonathan Schell. Wallace, in due course, found his way. He became a well-known actor and playwright. Though he wrote in the highest, most meticulous prose style his work included references to insects, violence, blood, obscenity, disease. He went, in other words, in directions almost absolutely at odds with the tastes and nearly phobic aversions of his father. In those days, he was not yet a success. His plays were unpublished. He had no acting jobs. He was unknown and poor. The choice of Jonathan Schell, and the exclusion of Wallace, seemed to me to be motivated by something more complex than the best interests of the magazine.

I was in my house in Newtown, then, a law school student, out of the *New Yorker* loop, one evening, when the phone rang. Jonathan Schell. "They have fired Mr. Shawn," he said.

I said I didn't quite believe it. Mr. Schell said that it was so.

"As surely as Ford fired Lee Iacocca," he said, "they have fired Mr. Shawn."

I said I still could not believe it. As the conversation went on, it seemed clear to me that the critical issue was still Mr. Shawn's choice of Mr. Schell as his successor. I said, "Jonathan, can you not separate the question of your succession from the question of whether or not Mr. Shawn has been fired?"

"Can you separate Hitler," Jonathan asked, "from the dismemberment of Czechoslovakia?"

So the terms of the discussion were set. From then on, Mr. Schell and Lillian Ross began to refer to Gardner Botsford (of all people) as Hitler, and to Gardner's wife, Janet Malcolm (again, of all people) as Lady Macbeth. They said that Gardner had persuaded his step-brother Peter Fleischmann to appoint him editor. They said that Gardner and Janet had engineered a coup to make *Janet* editor. This was bizarre, insanely out of character. Recently, Ms. Malcolm, who did not know, at the time, that she and Mr. Botsford were being characterized in this way, asked, sensibly, why Lady Macbeth, why not Mrs. Hitler, or Eva Braun? I could not say. The word *evil* was about. I thought this melodrama was a sign that Mr. Shawn was getting old.

Mr. Shawn was usually a gentle presence and a highly honorable man. He tried, usually, to keep his word. "I don't think I have anything to reproach myself for," I once heard him say to a writer who had disagreed with him on some minor matter. I thought the sentence was characteristic of him. He tried, and nearly succeeded, to live in such a way that he never had, or never thought he had, anything to reproach himself for. The only way he could break his word, within his code of honor, was to forget he had given it. Increasingly, over the years, that is what he did. During three periods, in my years at *The New Yorker,* I had reason to see

Mr. Shawn almost every day. Only one of these sequences had anything to do with me or my work. My respect for Mr. Shawn was so deep that I thought, for a time, I must have misunderstood what was said, or that my memory had completely failed me—so radically at odds were some of our conversations with what I thought had been said, or agreed, a few days, or even one day, before. I began to write scripts for myself, on the nights before I went to his office. When I got home from a visit, I would write down what I thought he and I had just said. There was no doubt about it. Sometimes the differences were just shadings. Often they went well beyond distortion to an almost comic contradiction of what actually occurred. In all the time I knew him, I never mentioned these contradictions. It would have been like Gerry's having asked to meet the fateful "they." I was afraid to make him angry. I didn't care for personal confrontations any more than he did. It occurred to me that it might be inevitable, over time, for the leader of any large enterprise—particularly a leader as acutely sensitive as Mr. Shawn to what people needed or wanted to hear—to acquire a habit of saying, or promising, something, and promptly forgetting it. You cannot, I think, have too good a memory and run a weekly. I came to believe that these inconsistencies, this duplicity, these lapses of memory, were an essential element of Mr. Shawn's way of running the magazine.

After all these years, it turns out that Gardner Botsford, too, felt obliged, at one period, to keep memos of what he and Mr. Shawn actually said. There was, of course, no coup.

Mr. Shawn, in the aftermath of his own efforts, which he sometimes fiercely defended, sometimes denied, to appoint Jonathan Schell, had told Mr. Botsford that he was tired of these struggles, that it would relieve him of some of his burden if Mr. Botsford would consent to an interim appointment as his successor. Gardner, touched, and against his better judgment, agreed. Whereupon Mr. Shawn rounded upon him, denounced him in a letter to the publisher, Peter Fleischmann, and began, with Lillian Ross and Jonathan Schell, his embittered campaign. Then Mr. Botsford, hurt and offended by accusations that he had been, in effect, dishonorable, disloyal, and, for that matter, unable to run the magazine, became angered in turn. There were scenes. There was an exchange of angry letters. Mr. Shawn remained editor. But what can have been the point? Why maneuver someone into an agreement, which he himself was not going to honor, and by which he was to become, apparently genuinely, enraged?

The problem, I think, had begun ten years earlier. In 1967, when Mr. Shawn published "The Village of Ben Suc," a two-part piece by Jonathan Schell. Mr. Schell had written the piece after ten days in Vietnam, on accreditation from *The Harvard Crimson.* This set in motion what became a crisis—which lasted until the end of Mr. Shawn's tenure and, to a considerable extent, brought the end of that tenure about. Mr. Schell was soon writing many of the magazine's Notes & Comment pieces, about Vietnam, disarmament, various issues. Mr. Shawn had sometimes called

Notes & Comment "the voice of the magazine." With Jonathan Schell's pieces, he began to call it "the conscience of the magazine." People claim to find at various points the beginning of the decline of *The New Yorker.* Some people trace it to the publication, in 1970, of "The Greening of America," a piece by Charles Reich, which had a kind of absurd, Forrest Gump sunniness and optimism. That piece became a best-selling book. It could be defended. I believe the decline really set in when *The New Yorker* began to move, consistently, predictably, piously, and joylessly, to the Left.

The leftward tilt, especially in Notes & Comment, had its roots in *New Yorker* tradition, going back at least to E. B. White and his fervent support of World Federalism. I am a fan of *Charlotte's Web* and *Stuart Little.* I have never cared for White's political or moral instincts, as expressed in Talk of the Town.

By the late nineteen sixties, *The New Yorker* was addressing genuine moral issues—in its very solid reporting, on civil rights, for example, from the South. There were valuable pieces by thoughtful contrarians—Edward Jay Epstein, Leopold Tyrmand, sometimes William Pfaff. But essentially, in my view, the magazine began to churn out volumes of what, even then, was politically correct propaganda and heavy preaching. Mr. Shawn and, to a lesser degree, Ms. Ross were spending more and more of their time with Mr. Schell.

It was in the nature of *New Yorker* contracts, under

Shawn, that they were not really contracts. A typical agreement would consist of four points. In the first, *The New Yorker* agreed to pay into the writer's account with the magazine the sum of one hundred dollars, in consideration of signing the agreement. Quite often, the writer had no account with the magazine, so that provision was meaningless. In the next, the magazine agreed to pay, for each accepted piece, a sum not less than a given amount per word. Contrary to a generally held notion that *The New Yorker* rewarded excessive length, the contract actually provided a bonus for brevity. In the third provision, the writer vaguely promised to devote his efforts to writing for the magazine. And then, depending on whether the contract was for fact or fiction, there was some vague fourth provision.

This contract, which was not a contract, since it obligated no one to anything, was often accompanied by an informal note from Mr. Shawn, expressing pleasure with the writer's work in the past year, or expressing a hope that he would write more in the following year. That was it. Except for the fact that writers were always paid at a rate higher than the rate stipulated in the agreement, it was impossible to know (except in cases like E. J. Kahn's, where a payment was once sent in error to a writer with a similar name) what anyone was paid, or even what one was going to be paid from one piece to the next. Also, contrary to widely held belief, the *New Yorker* pay scale was not particularly high. Mr. Shawn paid any writer, for any given piece, what he felt like paying.

Unless he chose to pay a sum many times what was stipulated in the contract, or unless a writer published an unusually high number of pieces in a single year, this was not a living wage.

One anomaly, however, was that Talk of the Town pieces, particularly Notes & Comment, were paid at a higher rate, proportionally, than pieces in any other section of the magazine. The reason for this was partly the voice-of-the-magazine aspect, and partly a bonus for anonymity, for the writer's forgoing the use of his own name. The writer of very frequent pieces was sure to be highly paid. In the days of Elizabeth Drew's Letters from Washington, it was plausibly rumored that she was the most highly paid contributor in the history of the magazine. A writer of very frequent Notes & Comment was certain to be, in comparison with most other staff writers, very well paid indeed. For this reason, among others—including his high moral, some would say moralistic tone; his time spent with Mr. Shawn and clear status as the favorite; his imitation of Mr. Shawn, in personal style and even in the inflections of his speech; and finally, the impression that things said among the writers themselves were reported by him to Mr. Shawn—led to reservations, with ingredients of envy and fear, about Mr. Schell. When Mr. Shawn began to send him pieces to edit, and Mr. Schell turned out to have no particular gift for it, the writers affected immediately expressed their outrage and dismay. Mr. Shawn withdrew his proposal that Mr.

Schell succeed him, and denied that he had ever made such a proposal. Then came the union crisis.

Some members of the staff, mostly young, invited the Guild to unionize the office. The Guild was a mean, bumbling union, which had already incurred a number of failures for its membership in long, nasty, costly, and ineffective strikes at newspapers, including *The New York Times.* While many on *The New Yorker* staff—the men in makeup, for example, and the secretaries—were underpaid in comparison with their counterparts at other magazines, these were not the people who had invited the union to come in. The invitation came from people whose jobs were amorphous and undefined (like my assignment years before to read books and see "whether there might be something for us" in them), and who had been hired on the chance that they would find their talents in due course. As a legal matter, however, as soon as such an invitation to a union is made, and until after a vote is taken, management is prohibited from expressing to labor either "promises of benefits" or "threats of reprisal." At *The New Yorker,* it was difficult even to define "management." Were editors management? Probably. But they were among the underpaid, putative members of the union. If the union came in, all the amorphous jobs, not to speak of Mr. Shawn's powers to pay what he liked, would disappear. Mr. Shawn was hurt and enraged. Bosses often are. But Mr. Schell seemed at least equally enraged. He seemed to encourage Mr. Shawn in his anger. In a writer published, and paid, as frequently as Mr. Schell, this seemed to reflect a lack of sympathy and imagination.

Bill Whitworth stepped in. With great tact and sensitivity, and with enormous patience, he produced a miracle. At his urging, and before any vote was taken, those who had invited the union withdrew their request. In the annals of labor relations, this is almost unheard of. The inviters asked in return only that Mr. Shawn agree to meet, from time to time, with a staff committee, to discuss grievances. Mr. Schell expressed his view that this was a capitulation and a betrayal. Mr. Shawn and Ms. Ross appeared to share that view. It became clear that, if Mr. Whitworth had ever been a candidate for the succession, he no longer was. Years later, Mortimer Zuckerman bought *The Atlantic Monthly*. Mr. Whitworth's reputation among writers, by then, was so high that Mr. Zuckerman offered him the editorship. Mr. Whitworth went to see Mr. Shawn. He had been living in a fairly poor apartment, in a not very safe neighborhood, with his wife, an adolescent son, and a baby daughter. He needed a raise. He told Mr. Shawn about the offer from Mr. Zuckerman. Mr. Shawn advised him not to take it. He did not offer a raise. A few months later, Mr. Zuckerman made the offer again. Mr. Whitworth went to see Mr. Shawn. His wife had threatened to leave him unless he got a raise. The adolescent son was growing up in the not safe neighborhood. He did not, Mr. Whitworth said, want to leave *The New Yorker*. Mr. Shawn replied that he should not leave, that *The Atlantic* had no future. He did not mention a raise. Mr. Whitworth took the job at *The Atlantic.* (It is likely that he would have been a far better editor of *The New Yorker.*) Stephen Fleischmann, the magazine's publisher, wrote Whitworth that he was "a fucking idiot" to leave. Mr. Shawn gave his remaining editors a raise.

In 1982, *The New Yorker* published "The Fate of the Earth," by Jonathan Schell, a five-part meditation on nuclear war. When the pieces were published in book form, by Knopf, the jacket copy, unsigned, was written in fact by Mr. Shawn. He described the book as "possibly one of the great events in the history of human thought." Even given the occasionally effusive nature of jacket copy, this seemed excessive. But Mr. Shawn, whose last published piece (apart from some very concise and moving obituaries of *New Yorker* writers) was thought to have been a little fantasy about a meteor's hitting New York, in 1945, had actually been writing several Notes & Comments himself since Mr. Schell came to the magazine. His views often echoed Mr. Schell's. When *The Fate of the Earth* was published in Germany, a reviewer raised a question of plagiarism. Certain points and passages in the book, particularly a chapter called "The Second Death," closely resembled parts of a book originally published in Germany—written, in fact, by a former husband of Hannah Arendt.

Mr. Schell flew to Germany to bring suit. He said he had never read the book. He said that it had never been published in English, and that he did not read German. He threatened lawsuits against *Newsweek* and other publications that mentioned the matter—including *The New Republic,* which was edited by then by Hendrik Hertzberg, his former colleague at *The New Yorker.* Mr. Hertzberg denied that a suit was ever threatened. "We are friends," he said, "and friends do not sue each other." The earlier book, it turned out, had indeed been published in English. A few other publications explored the matter. Then it gradually faded from memory. It assumed its place at the end of a complicated series of *New Yorker* scandals and non-scandals, between 1975 and 1979, which Mr. Shawn had inexplicably combined, and indignantly dismissed—to the great detriment of the magazine.

In the late seventies, Alastair Reid, a fine poet and translator, had published in *The New Yorker* several Letters from a Spanish Village. *The New Yorker* had had, for decades, a sensible, jovial, perhaps overly cautious lawyer, Milton Greenstein. Before publishing the "Yma Dream" story, for example, Mr. Greenstein had actually required Tom Meehan to obtain, in writing, the permission of everyone whose name appeared in it—a process that took more than a year. In 1967, Mr. Greenstein had cut from a piece of mine, about a radical convention in Chicago, a description of a hotel as having "gusty arctic air-conditioning and dark, depressing rooms." "There is no doubt that it's opinion," he said. "It's protected by the First Amendment. But it's also not worth getting sued." In what may have been his own debacle regarding succession, Mr. Greenstein had brought in a young lawyer, Joseph Cooper, who did not have Mr. Greenstein's instincts or his skills. In his capacity as a *New Yorker* person, Mr. Cooper agreed to teach a seminar at Yale. He invited Alastair Reid to address the seminar. At one point, Mr. Reid said that the reporter's art had an element of fiction—that he, for example, had made up a tavern, and some other scenes, in one of his Letters from a Spanish Village. Lawyers, of course, are supposed not to create, but to preclude, occasions for clients to make admissions of this kind. Mr. Cooper, who had his own aspirations as a writer, permitted Mr. Reid to expand on these remarks. One of the students in the seminar went on, after graduation, to take a job at *The Wall Street Journal,* where she published a story based on what Mr. Reid had said. That night, Bill Whitworth called me in Newtown, from his office at *The Atlantic.*

"Tell Mr. Shawn, or get word to him somehow," he said, "that he'd better not defend Alastair in this." I called Lillian Ross. I told her what Mr. Whitworth said.

"He doesn't know what he's talking about," she said. "And you don't either." She hung up.

Mr. Shawn did try to defend Mr. Reid—with the result that the story went on, day after day, with articles that included an editorial in *The New York Times.* The notion that it is all right to make stories up and present them as nonfiction was, of course, indefensible. That Mr. Shawn should try to defend it was damaging to *The New Yorker*—which, until that incident, was trusted, almost above all, for the accuracy of its reporting. There are elements in all published journalism that necessarily reflect an element of fiction. Quotations that appear in print, for example, are hardly ever verbatim. The rhythms of actual speech transcribed would make most stories endless. A usable authentic verbatim quote virtually leaps from the page, so rare is it among the sentences that appear lamely between quotation marks. If stories were to include as well the question and answer that actually produce what is quoted, hardly any story, in any newspaper or magazine, would be readable at all. That said—that there is a difference between stenography and reporting—it is all the more crucial that every non-fiction story be, fundamentally (that is, literally, and not metaphorically, or at a "deeper" level; fiction is the place for metaphorical or "deeper" truths) true. It was no service to Mr. Reid, certainly, to keep this lapse perpetually in print.

Not long after this crisis, however, there occurred another. Two incidents, actually, which Mr. Shawn managed to elide, in a particularly damaging way. The first concerned an article by Penelope Gilliatt, a profile of Graham Greene. Ms. Gilliatt was one of the magazine's two film critics. (The other was Pauline Kael.) Over the years, Mr. Shawn had several times been put on notice that Ms. Gilliatt plagiarized. In this instance, the checkers had noticed that Ms. Gilliatt's piece tracked, to an extraordinary degree, an article in *The Nation,* by Michael Mewshaw. They had called this to Mr. Shawn's attention. He called it to the attention of Ms. Gilliatt. She was incensed. Of course, she said, Graham Greene had said to Mr. Mewshaw the same sort of things he said to her—evidence not of plagiarism but of accuracy. This did not quite meet the facts. Her profile tracked Mr. Mewshaw's in details that could not have come from Graham Greene. After a tirade or two from Ms. Gilliatt, Mr. Shawn made his decision. He ran the piece. Within days, he received a letter from Mr. Greene. A lot of the piece, Mr. Greene said, was pure, even mad, invention. He gave three examples. Ms. Gilliatt wrote that, as she interviewed Mr. Greene in Monte Carlo, vultures were flying overhead. There were, Mr. Greene said, no vultures in Monte Carlo. She mentioned watching with him, on BBC television, an interview with some Bulgarians. He had not watched any television with Ms. Gilliatt, and there had been no such program on the BBC. She quoted him about "concentration camps in Argentina." He had never spoken of concentration camps in Argentina, and he did not know of any. Mr. Shawn did not reply to this letter. Mr. Greene published it in *The New Statesman. The Los Angeles Times* picked it up. Mr. Mewshaw had meanwhile raised his claim of plagiarism.

At approximately the same time, John McPhee, a scrupulous and highly respected reporter, published in *The New Yorker* a piece about a restaurant and its chef, to whom he gave the pseudonym "Otto." Mr. McPhee said that this restaurant was one of the finest he knew, that it was within driving distance of New York, and that he would not divulge its name, because "Otto" did not wish to be written about, and because Mr. McPhee himself did not wish the restaurant to be spoiled by crowds. There was something uncharacteristically unprofessional, even spiteful, in a mystification of this sort. Mr. Shawn initially justified his publication of the piece by saying that *The New Yorker* agreed to conceal the name of the chef, and of his restaurant, because the magazine never published pieces about people who did not want to be written about. If "Otto" did not wish to be written about, of course, Mr. McPhee need not have written about him. There were other difficulties. Mr. McPhee said that "Otto" occasionally served a delicacy that could not be obtained elsewhere: fresh sea urchin. Sushi bars, which had sprung up all over New York, were daily serving fresh sea urchin. And Mr. McPhee quoted "Otto" to the effect that—unlike Lutèce—his restaurant never served frozen fish. Lutèce submitted to *The New Yorker* its invoices for fresh fish, and threatened to sue.

What Mr. Shawn did was to defend Ms. Gilliatt's piece and Mr. McPhee's, as though they presented comparable issues. Then the magazine apologized to Lutèce for the allegations about frozen fish. Mr. McPhee's piece was well within the limits of professionalism. (Invoices for any number of fresh fish do not prove that frozen fish were *never* served; the apology may have been unnecessary.) Ms. Gilliatt's was not. Mr. Shawn put Ms. Gilliatt on indefinite leave, for any pieces except fiction. He authorized payments to Mr. Mewshaw. But his underlying contentions, that *The New Yorker,* in both cases, and in Mr. Reid's, was completely right, undermined the magazine's reputation. He became enmeshed in a notion of infallibility, of misplaced moral certitude, and began to cast doubt on just those areas where the magazine was genuinely strong.

At this time, Mr. Shawn undertook an almost reflexive defense of his decisions and of everything that appeared in the magazine. He began to doubt the good faith of anyone who disagreed with him. In particular, Mr. Shawn began to believe that he and the magazine were being pursued vindictively by *The New York Times,* and its editor A. M. Rosenthal. This was remarkable for two reasons. The *Times* was probably the only publication in those years that maintained its standards, its excellence and its reliability, as firmly as did *The New Yorker.* The *Times,* under Mr. Rosenthal, had reason to think that *The New Yorker* was vindictively pursuing the *Times.* Especially in the Talk of the Town, *The New Yorker* routinely used stories from the *Times,* without any sort of credit or attribution. The *Times* was so dependable in those days that *The New Yorker* may have looked upon news derived from it as Revealed Truths, which did not require credit. To reporters and editors at the *Times,* the practice was galling. Far worse: The space and time *The New Yorker* offered its writers for research and thinking sometimes made the *Times,* along with other publications under news deadline pressure, look ridiculous. A few *New Yorker* writers were especially proficient at the analysis, and demolition, of news stories, as well as any form of conventional wisdom or received ideas. In 1971, in an article called "The Panther and the Police: A Pattern of Genocide?" Edward Jay Epstein examined the notion, almost universally believed, that police, across the United States, had killed thirteen Black Panthers. Charles Garry, lawyer for the Panthers had said so. Journalists took it up. Everyone believed it. Mr. Epstein looked at the matter case by case, and discovered that, of the alleged thirteen, some were not dead and most of the rest were not Panthers. One was an apple vendor who died, of natural causes, beside his apple cart. The piece was valuable and important. It probably saved lives. The police themselves had come to believe in these killings. They had also come to believe that killing was what had kept the Panthers under control. For journalists, an attack by another journalist seems to provoke unusual fury. A piece like Mr. Epstein's was humiliating. With the *Times* attacking *The New Yorker*, editorially, on such issues as the Alastair Reid case, and *The New Yorker* upsetting the *Times*, in the matter of Panthers, each of these institutions, which otherwise had so much in common, was convinced that it was the victim of persecution by the other.

In time, after the second unsuccessful attempt to install Mr. Schell, and the demonization of Ms. Malcolm and Mr. Botsford, Ms. Ross found William McKibben, a writer for *The Harvard Crimson*. Mr. Shawn hired him as a writer, and he became the next candidate for the succession. By then, it had become clear to many of us that Mr. Shawn did not want a successor, and that his choice of candidates who were unacceptable for one reason or another was no accident. But there was bitterness about the matter, in all its meaningless and acrimonious stages, from the early seventies until at least 1987, when Mr. Shawn left the magazine.

On Christmas Eve, 1973, I received a phone call from John Doar, an old friend from the days of the Civil Rights marches in the South. Mr. Doar, head of the Civil Rights Division of the Justice Department in the last days of the Eisenhower administration, and then under Presidents Kennedy and Johnson, had been a hero of the sixties. In a famous incident, just after the murder, in Mississippi, of Medgar Evers, a procession of black mourners was walking down the street in one direction, Mississippi troopers were advancing toward them in the other. Jeering white mobs were on the sidelines. The troopers had lowered their bayonets. Bricks and bottles were flying overhead. Reporters had dropped to the trenches at the roadside. Mr. Doar, arms raised, crossed the road between the mourners and the troopers.

"My name is John Doar," he said. "And everyone around here knows I stand for what is right." He turned to the troopers and asked them to turn away their bayonets. He turned to the black mourners and said, very slowly, "You can't win it in the streets."

There was no violence that day. For years afterward, Mr. Doar's division brought lawsuits, and patiently compiled records of the abuses that led, in part, to the Voter Registration Act of 1965. The anomaly was this: Mr. Doar, having served under Eisenhower, was a Republican, although he had served, for most of his time in the division, under Democratic presidents.

"Now, you're a Republican," Mr. Doar said, in his phone call on Christmas Eve. That was true. I had registered as a Republican because I wanted to vote against Barry Goldwater, and for Nelson Rockefeller, in the primary of 1964. In the early days of political correctness, I liked to imagine as well that I was the only Republican reporter, not just on the staff of *The New Yorker*, but in New York. "I think you could be fair." He asked me to come to Washington, for a job on the impeachment inquiry of the Judiciary Committee of the House of Representatives. He did not feel free, on the telephone, to say in what capacity I would work there, or for how long. I did not feel that I had to ask Mr. Shawn for permission, or for a leave of absence. *The New Yorker* had been so absolutely and consistently anti-Nixon for so long that I was sure he would have no objection. I did ask him, though, whether I could write about it, one day, for the magazine. He said I could.

When I went to Washington and spoke to Mr. Doar, it was clear that every important element of the inquiry was to be, for the inquiry's duration, secret. Afterwards, I would be free to write about it. Mr. Doar had read what material there was on the subject of impeachment of a president. There was not much: essentially just the writings of the Framers, and a book by the constitutional scholar Raoul Berger. Doar had concluded that, to the degree impeachment is warranted, it would be wise—given the powers of the president and thc fact that the underlying offense, if any, is certain to have to do with the abuse of just those powers—to be less than open about the process. He had also concluded that President Nixon should be impeached. In interviewing lawyers for his staff, he intended to ask them whether they had any views whatever as to whether the president ought to be impeached. If they did, he would not hire them. He was going to hire an equal number of Democrats and Republicans, but he was not going to allow an appearance of a "tilt" either way. Anyone who was not, by late 1973, tilting one way or the other on the question of impeachment was likely to have been living in considerable isolation. The lawyers he would hire, I assumed, would be savvy enough to conceal their views. Hillary Rodham was, of course, one lawyer Doar hired. Bernard Nussbaum was another. Bill Clinton, who was running at the time for attorney general of Arkansas, came to visit. My job, at the outset, was to write the speeches of Chairman Peter Rodino. He was not to know who was writing them. Nor was anyone else. Mr. Doar did not believe that speechwriters, like Theodore Sorenson, Emmett Hughes, or Richard Goodwin, served anyone's interests by going public. The chairman, however, must have the Quotation of the Day in the *Times* every time he spoke. This was no small thing. It would be hard to produce words worth quoting, over a period of some months, when the rule for the substance was that it could not tilt.

Mr. Rodino's first major speech was to be a request that the House grant his committee, for its inquiry, the subpoena power. Mr. Doar said he would like the chairman to inspire the House to act honorably by recalling historic moments, in the past, when Congress had acted nobly. Back in New York, I called Martin Duberman, a writer and a respected historian at Columbia. I asked him for those instances of fine conduct by Congress in the past. He thought about it. It seemed there were not any. The chairman, in that first speech, quoted Edmund Burke. (It had taken a last flurry of research to prove that the remarks in question, eloquent and harmless in themselves, were not from Burke's impeachment of Warren Hastings.) He got the Quotation of the Day—that day, and for most of his major speeches later. He told reporters that he had always been a student of Edmund Burke. My job evolved.

The inquiry had to produce strategies and voluminous documents of all sorts, and Mr. Doar had increasingly to rely on the writing, thinking, and editing of friends he had known and trusted long before the inquiry began. These were Burke Marshall, a professor at the Yale Law School, who had been Mr. Doar's boss at the Justice Department; Owen Fiss, a professor at the University of Chicago Law School, who had worked for Mr. Doar in the division; Robert Owen, a New York lawyer, who had been Doar's deputy in the division; Dorothy Shelton, who had worked for him there as well; and me. There was also one newcomer, Robert Shelton, who had been a lawyer with the National Security Agency. Mr. Shelton became an invaluable member of the staff, but he, too, was not really a stranger. He was Ms. Shelton's older brother.

For the months from January to August 1976, when President Nixon resigned, I virtually lost contact with *The New Yorker*—except for this: I learned to edit, and to copy-edit, the volumes of text that were produced, every day, by the inquiry, and printed, overnight, by the Government Printing Office. I discovered that I had learned this from Mr. Shawn, that I genuinely liked it, and that I could do it—this part was surprising to me—without making the writers unhappy. I had been through the editing process, on the writer's side. It was clear to me that writers of even the most obscure inquiry documents cared more about what they had written than I did. There was no conflict of wills. In any revision, the writer had to be happy with it. Shawn's example of anonymity, silence, and discretion was also helpful. Better than a pseudonym, I also discovered, was writing words for someone else. Elizabeth Arden. Peter Rodino. All anxiety recedes. I don't think speechwriters are ever subject to writer's block. When I returned to the magazine, however, I realized that my absence in Washington—like my absence six years before, when I went to the *Times*—appeared to some members of the staff, including friends, including perhaps Ms. Ross and even Mr. Shawn—as "mandarin" behavior, too much in the world, even selling out.

My time in Washington had at least two lasting results. The first was that I formed, at first, a speculation, then a certainty about what had really been the issue in Watergate. I did some research, and then wrote a piece. Mr. Shawn considered it for a long time, said that he was persuaded by it and agreed with it, but also said he could not publish it. I understood that. The piece argued, and to a degree demonstrated, that there was, indeed, in Watergate a form of "treason," as contemplated in the constitutional phrase "Treason, Bribery, or other High Crimes and Misdemeanors"—that it had to do with the China Lobby, the war in Vietnam, and foreign campaign contributions. By the time the piece appeared, in *The Atlantic Monthly* (then still under the editorship of Robert Manning and Michael Janeway), I was in law school.

Another upshot, for me, of my time in Washington was an idea for *The New Yorker*, not for a piece but for a department. It was not unusual for Mr. Shawn to create new departments. He had devised Reflections, for contemplative pieces that did not fit in any other category. He once gave me a column called Other Events, for reviews of events that did not strictly fall within any conventional category of performance. I wrote one Other Events column, and then gave it up. He once turned an account I had written of the Meredith march into a Notes & Comment, and ran it for the entirety of Talk of the Town. The department I had in mind, however, was broad. It might even consist of two departments. I had noticed that, while elected officials and administrations come and go, certain governmental bureaucracies remain. The General Accounting Office, the General Services Administration, even the Government Printing Office are among the least reported on, least understood, and certainly among the most important. At the same time, some of the most revealing, and vital, reporting on government is done by the government itself—in its unending flow of reports from the Government Printing Office. The reporting convention, at newspapers and magazines, was, and is—those were the days of Woodward and Bernstein, and Sy Hersh—to interview two people, two "sources," and if they bear each other out, to run the story. When a government institution—the Church Committee on Intelligence, for example—issues a report, which commonly runs to several volumes and to many thousands of pages, the convention is to run with the accompanying press release. No reporter has the time or patience or temperament to wade through those documents. So the conventions exist: either the press release, or the word of two living sources.

The department, or two departments, that I had in mind would report, first, on those perdurable bureaucracies, in Profile, one after another. Each of them was, almost unarguably, more powerful and more important than any of Washington's transient personalities. Second, the magazine would report in detail on those documents by which the government reports upon itself. For this work, the ideal staff would be recent graduates of universities, who had been trained in reading and research. Those graduates, when they look for jobs as writers or editors, are commonly told that they don't have the experience for it. The question for them is, naturally, how in the absence of such experience they can ever get the jobs in which the experience is to be had. The government documents in question are long, often poorly written, always repetitious. A scholar, trained a bit in what to look for (more important, perhaps, trained in what to skip) could glean, and turn out, valuable material unavailable through any other source. He could either pass it on to established reporters, or write it up, and become a reporter himself—accustomed to rely not on gossip from two, possibly lying, possibly agreeing by prearrangement, and thus amounting really to a single source and an accomplice, almost certainly self-interested living "sources," but on government documents.

"It is not that easy," Mr. Shawn said. There had to be an idea of what to look for. He said that a department, or departments, of this sort could add a valuable category of reporting, which could contribute to journalism of every other kind. It would be a kind of antidote to television reporting. He liked the idea of having a new reason to hire young people, those recent graduates for research. He understood every possible implication. He thought the project could begin in *The New Yorker*, but, once it was established, grow too large. *The New Yorker* had introduced new standards and conventions for reporting before. Then, he said, "Before we establish a department, why don't you try writing just one piece?" It became a sort of joke. I interviewed the heads of the G.S.A. and the G.A.O. My house filled with documents

Judge Sirica ✗

from agencies. Working on my own, I found it hopeless. We were stuck right there. I went back to work on fiction.

At one point, it occurred to me that two dramas within the Watergate story had been left entirely unresolved. One was the incident of Yeoman Radford, Admiral Moorer, and the Joint Chiefs of Staff—rifling a briefcase and otherwise spying on Henry Kissinger in the course of Dr. Kissinger's overtures to and trips to China. The other had to do with G. Gordon Liddy. At law school, I had begun to have serious back trouble. I was in and out of hospitals. I just did not seem to have the energy to pursue the Yeoman Radford story. My mother's house, however, was in Danbury, Connecticut. Mr. Liddy was in the Danbury federal penitentiary. When he was caught in the Watergate burglary, Mr. Liddy had burned the cash. Burning cash is an extremely powerful image. Cash is burned, for instance, in the fireplace in *The Brothers Karamazov*. Mr. Liddy, alone among the burglars, had stayed silent. I took it into my head that Mr. Liddy's silence was a sign, not just of loyalty, or stoicism, but that he knew a lot. Mr. Shawn had given me, for review, a book by the Watergate judge, John Sirica. In the course of research, I had found that, contrary to what he wrote, and contrary to his reputation as a hero, Sirica was in fact a corrupt, incompetent, and dishonest figure, with a close connection to Senator Joseph McCarthy and clear ties to organized crime. I did not review the book.

I wrote to Mr. Liddy, though, saying that I was at work on an article for *The New Yorker;* I was in Danbury. He was in

Danbury. I wondered whether, after all this time, he might answer some questions. In his reply, Mr. Liddy wrote, very courteously, that he had vowed to himself never to discuss the matter. I wrote back to say that I understood, and I thanked him for his reply. He wrote back and thanked me for my note of thanks. There seemed nothing left for me to do, except to bake him a pie with a file in it. He was released, briefly, from prison, for a press conference in Washington. He invited me. I wrote back to say I had back trouble and did not know whether I could go. He wrote, saying that if I had back trouble, I should by no means risk a trip to Washington.

I did go. A mistake. The press conference was about prison conditions. There had been a fire at the federal prison in Danbury. Several inmates had died. The press swarmed, with Mr. Liddy, into one small room of a hotel suite. Because of my back trouble, I found it difficult to stand. I went to an adjoining bedroom and phoned for a taxi to National Airport. I went back to Danbury. Three days later, a letter from Mr. Liddy. He had been relieved, he said to think I had not come to that farcical press conference. I must imagine his chagrin when he later learned that "a blonde, in obvious agony," had been lying on the bed in the next room. I wrote, again, to say that I was not a blonde, that I had not been in agony, and to thank him for his concern. That was that. He published a thriller, which I thought pretty good. Then, his autobiography appeared.

At that time—it was 1979—Jimmy Carter was president. There were hostages in Teheran. I asked Mr. Shawn if I could accompany Mr. Liddy on his book tour and write a piece to be called "G. Gordon Liddy in America." He saw it at once. On a book tour, to cities, towns, radio stations, television stations, land grant colleges, an America was likely to reveal itself in response to Mr. Liddy which would be different from the country one would encounter with anyone else, or in any other way. Mr. Liddy's autobiography was, beyond doubt, a writer's biography—a writer of some sensitivity and talent. Mr. Liddy himself had not taken on the role he has played subsequently—or, for all I know, that he may have played before his time in prison. He was moderate, polite, intelligent, somewhat prone to minor disasters and contretemps. On his first day on the circuit, for example, he had, all stoicism aside, such a toothache that I took him to my dentist, who was somewhat surprised to have him as a patient. At nearly every stop along the tour, the car ordered for him by his publisher failed, for one reason or another, to show up. He was devoted to his wife and his four children—each of them interesting, not one in any sense a clone of any of the others—and determined to make up to them for the disruption he had caused in their lives. The lecture bureau that ran his schedule consisted of two young men, who seemed to have no idea of the stamina required, over the long haul, to fly one day to Montana, the next to Georgia, the third to Maine, then back to North Dakota, then perhaps to Kentucky. To land grant colleges, TV stations, business groups. I flew back to New York, I wrote my piece. Mr. Shawn scheduled it for publication within the month.

Suddenly, it was no longer scheduled. For the first and only time, I asked Mr. Shawn a question on this subject. Was it merely postponed, or would it never run? "This has never happened before," he said. "There was an uprising. I had to yield." Well, all right, I thought. One is never that certain about a piece. I went back to fiction. I turned in a story. Mr. Shawn praised it, set it in type, scheduled it, and unscheduled it again. That had happened to me, from time to time, over the years. Sometimes the stories ran in the end, sometimes not. It happened with yet another story. I was losing hope. In the meantime, I had published a piece in the *New York Times Book Review*—a review of *The Brethren,* Bob Woodward and Scott Armstrong's book on the Supreme Court. I had not cared for the book. I had also had one of those experiences with the *Book Review* that makes one determined never to write for them again. Mr. Shawn had liked the review. He sent me a check, for fifteen hundred dollars. A surprising man—to send one a check for a piece in another publication. On the other hand, in that period of scheduling and unscheduling pieces and stories, it was the only check I received from him.

One day in 1981, *The New York Review* sent me, for review, the most recent book by Pauline Kael. I had been sitting out there in the country. I started to read. The next day,

I called Bill Whitworth—Ms. Kael's editor and sometimes mine.

"Tell me," I said, "why I shouldn't write a really negative review of Pauline Kael's book."

"Because you like her work," he said.

"That's true," I said. It was true. I had always liked her work. Bill and I talked about other matters, and hung up. I read more of the book. I called Bill again.

"I used to like her work," I said, "but now it's everything I detest about writing."

"Not everything," Bill said.

"What do you mean, Not everything?" I asked.

"Well," he said, "she's not a limousine liberal." That was true. There had been decades of limousine liberals. Pauline Kael was not one of them.

I finished the book. I began to brood about it. I have always felt that it isn't fair to write mean reviews about the frail or powerless, to level heavy guns at first novels by unknown writers or at the work of a poet in his garret. But Ms. Kael, far from being powerless, was a dominant, even domineering presence in film reviewing, and even in university film departments. She seemed to take particular pleasure in ridiculing small filmmakers (the Maysles come to mind; Merchant and Ivory; Claude Lanzmann, the director of *Shoah*). I could not understand why Mr. Shawn would run, as criticism, in the magazine after all of Edmund Wilson and Harold Rosenberg, piece after piece that violated, I believed, the limits not just of what *The New Yorker* should publish, but of what any decent magazine should publish, ad hominem, ad personam, inaccurate, sneering, mean. I thought Ms. Kael had become the leader of a posse of sycophants and bullies. I wrote my piece. It ran in *The New York Review*. Apostasy, apparently. Even Mr. Shawn took it hard, although Lillian Ross said he secretly agreed with me. Perhaps he did.

I had dinner with Donald Barthelme. He had once taken over *The New Yorker*'s film column (as I had) for a month, in a period when Ms. Kael had gone to Hollywood. He said that when people told him, in that month, how much they liked his film reviews, they always followed their compliments with a question: When's Pauline coming back? Now he said, "You've taken away her *language*. She'll tough it out. But you've taken away her language." I rather hoped I had. It seemed to me, looking back, that I had been pretty loyal to *The New Yorker*, defending—out of conviction, certainly, but all the same—the magazine and its writers (Hannah Arendt, John Updike, Donald Barthelme), attacking those whom it regarded as enemies (Herbert Gold, Tom Wolfe, and a group of hostile critics, in a long piece called "Polemic and the New Reviewers.") I went to birthday parties at the Shawns'. I saw Mr. Shawn frequently, in his office and in mine, and we discussed all sorts of questions. We had lunch, sometimes, at the Algonquin. He seemed to regard me as partly family, and partly as something of an explorer in the outside world.

I had close friends at the magazine, and yet it seemed obvious, to me if not to Mr. Shawn, that, for whatever reason, I had reached an impasse. I recalled two events from my first days at *The New Yorker.* Both concerned writers in our cohort. One had to do with William Wertenbaker, the other with Henry S. F. Cooper. Bill Wertenbaker, having submitted to *The New Yorker* a series of pieces that Mr. Shawn rejected, left to take a job at *Newsweek.* He worked there for two years. One day, as he was walking along the nineteenth-floor corridor on the way to lunch with a friend at the magazine, he met Mr. Shawn—who seemed very glad to see him. Where had Mr. Wertenbaker been? Mr. Shawn asked. Working on a long piece? He hoped so. "Well, not really," Bill said. He had been so busy at *Newsweek.* Mr. Shawn looked puzzled. *Newsweek*? Why was that? Bill explained that, after having so many pieces rejected, and not having heard from Mr. Shawn in a long time, he had assumed he had been fired. No, Mr. Shawn said, looking now dumbfounded. Mr. Wertenbaker came back to the magazine.

Henry Cooper had been a Talk reporter. He submitted a long piece. Nothing happened. No reply. He walked around, looking pale, for weeks, then gave up on that piece. Months later, he submitted another. No reply. Again, the weeks of waiting. Gerry Jonas said, This would not do. Henry must go to Mr. Shawn, tell him he realized that the piece had been rejected, and ask why, so that he could learn from the rejection, before he submitted his next piece. Henry went to see Mr. Shawn. No, no, Mr. Shawn said, the piece had certainly not been rejected. Mr. Cooper would be hearing from him soon. Weeks passed. Gerry said that Henry must again go to Mr. Shawn, say that now he knew for certain that the piece had been rejected, and again explain that he needed to find out why. Henry went again. Mr. Shawn again said, No, no, and assured Henry that he would soon hear definitely from him. Some weeks later, Henry received the piece, through the office mail, with one of the fuchsia slips, labeled *Urgent,* that were used at *The New Yorker* for inter-office communications of all kinds. The slip read: "To: Henry Cooper; From: William Shawn; Subject: For your files." This time, I thought I understood what had happened. Though I did not say so to Henry, I was certain that he had been fired—that Mr. Shawn, wishing to avoid the confrontation, had chosen this rather cruel way of letting Henry know. I was, as it turned out, wrong. Mr. Cooper became *The New Yorker*'s correspondent on all matters regarding Space. He published countless long pieces, through the years. They were first-rate pieces, too.

The impasse in my case seemed different. One piece after another (and I was not a prolific writer) was apparently generating what Mr. Shawn had called an uprising. That might, of course, have been his own way of saying that he did not like those pieces. He had, after all, the authority to override; he had overridden the judgment of his editors many times. But I did not think so. I did not mention my concern to anyone. I wondered whether the situation had been brought about, at least in part, by my review of Pauline Kael. On the same evening we discussed that piece, Donald Barthelme, who had been experiencing some difficulty with the fiction department, said, "You know Roger should edit *The New Yorker.* You ought to become fiction editor." The next day, Bill Whitworth said, "The magazine really needs another fiction editor. You ought to speak to Shawn." So I did. Mr. Shawn seemed as joyful as I had ever seen him. "Why, that's what we were going to do when you first came," he said. He said he had never liked the fiction department. "Roger is a good writer about baseball, and that's all I can say about it," he said. "You'll work with me. And I'm still here."

I should have known that it would never work. "They say the chemistry is wrong," he said, a few days later, "They say we'll have two fiction departments: them, and you and me." I saw that was true, and said so. I gave up on the idea. I wished I had never mentioned it.

Over the next weeks, Mr. Shawn called me in, with as many permutations of the plan for editing fiction as he had presented, years before, for the idea of a response in *The New Yorker* to the pieces by Tom Wolfe. I had learned, from that earlier experience, the certain outcome, in conversations with Mr. Shawn, when there had been any mention of a "they." He suggested that I edit non-fiction. *The New Yorker* had particularly strong editors in non-fiction; they were among the magazine's best and most hard-working people. I thanked him, and said no. I went back to writing fiction. In the meantime, Mr. Shawn resumed the game of the succession—Jonathan Schell; Bill McKibben; no one; a tandem effort: John Bennet together with Charles McGrath; Mr. McGrath alone; Mr. Bennet alone. John Bennet actually sold his house, to move nearer the city, in anticipation of his changed circumstances. The circumstances had not really changed.

In 1981, Mr. Shawn suddenly scheduled the piece that once was dead: "G. Gordon Liddy in America." I went to see him. I said, It would have been one thing to run the piece when Jimmy Carter was president, there were hostages in Teheran, and the president was, rather embarrassingly, carrying his own suitcase at airports and speaking of national malaise. It was quite another to schedule it during the presidency of Ronald Reagan, when the hostages had long since returned, the president was speaking of a City on a Hill, and even Gordon Liddy had begun to play a different role. When I wrote the piece, it was in some degree contrarian, to balance what I thought was one political consensus. Now that consensus was overbalanced, tilting quite the other way. Mr. Shawn said a piece was good or not, regardless of the political situation. I did not agree. I withdrew the piece.

I wrote a story, called "Orcas Island," and used a pseudonym. When I sent it to Mr. Shawn, he called within hours, and spoke of it as highly as I had heard him speak of anything. He asked whether I would drop the pseudonym. I said I preferred to keep it. He said, All right. He had used pseudonyms himself. He just wanted to send it through. A few days later, he called.

"It's very unfortunate," he said. "They know you wrote it."

"That's not so surprising," I said.

"They also said they know everybody in it," Mr. Shawn said.

"That can't be," I said. "It's fiction. Even if it were true, it would not just be philistine to reject fiction that is, in some sense, based on real characters. There wouldn't be any fiction.

"I know," he said. "They say they recognize everybody in it. They say everyone else will recognize them, because the portrayals are too real."

That was odd. Whatever "Orcas Island" was, if there was one genre to which it did not belong, that genre was realism. "Whom do they recognize?" I asked.

"I'm glad you asked that," Mr. Shawn said. "We had a Profile of him in the magazine. You called him Old Mush Mouth. Ramsey Clark."

I thought about that. There was one person in the story, identified as the attorney general of the United States. He was quoted in one line. In another line, a judge on the Fifth Circuit Court of Appeals, did call him Old Mush Mouth. The attorney general in question did exist. The line attributed to him had been quoted, from a press conference, by *The New York Times.* Judges on the Fifth Circuit Court of Appeals did call him Old Mush Mouth. There was nothing roman à clef about this. It was Griffin Bell.

"Oh," Mr. Shawn said. I withdrew the story. Late that night, he called. "We're going to run it. In the anniversary issue. If you'll just look at a few queries, you can address all their concerns. I've made the decision. I'm still here." I thought, I have heard this before. I worked on the story for a few months, addressing the concerns. I turned it in. Mr. Shawn said, "It's even better than it was. I'll put it through."

Early the next evening, I was having a drink, at the Coffee House, with Alastair Reid. Roger Angell came in. We asked him to join us. He said he was waiting for someone. He went to another table, sat down, and opened a newspaper. "I know all about it," Alastair said. "Roger told me, in the men's room. He said you turned in an awful story, and Shawn liked it. It almost went through. They think they've got it now. Chip and Veronica Geng have strangled it in its bassinet." That night, a friend on the staff of *Time* told me that a fiction editor at *The New Yorker* had called him to say that *The New Yorker* was about to publish, in a story by me, its first pornographic piece. I thought, This piece, without the slightest element of pornography, which I wished to publish under a pseudonym, is somehow becoming public and rejected, all at once.

That night, Mr. Shawn called. "It is fine," he said. "We are putting it right through."

A few days later, he called again. "It's very unfortunate," he said. "Underneath their queries, it turns out, there was a layer of their real objections. It's too hot. It's too sensational. The newspapers will take it up. And they say there have been too many imitators."

"Too many imitators," I said.

"Yes," he said. "It's a compliment to you, in a way." I withdrew the story again. I asked him to return it to me. Two nights later, Mr. Shawn called. "We've triumphed," he said. "I've made a few changes. They all agree. It will run. Come in tomorrow and look at the galleys. We'll send it through."

I came in the next morning. The story had become very long. Mr. Shawn had simply spliced in large sections of earlier stories that had been scheduled and unscheduled, and then had vanished. He had also cut, in a highly uncharacteristic way, so that, in spite of its new length, fragments of the most recent story were scattered and embedded in the rest. I spoke, I think, mildly. "It may seem that anything can go anywhere," I said, "but that doesn't really work."

"I know," Mr. Shawn said.

"And you've taken out everything you said you liked."

"I know," Mr. Shawn said. "Frankly, they weren't very enthusiastic about this version, either. But I got them to put it through." I thanked him. I withdrew the story yet again, and took it home.

Some weeks later, Mr. Shawn called me in. He had an idea, he said. He had taken all the stories of mine that had not run, and intercut them in such a way that they formed what he would run as a regular column, as yet untitled. It could run frequently. It would be fiction. And it would be my own. The fiction editors had agreed to this. He would be the editor. "You and I will work together, as we always have," he said. I was enormously touched. I looked at the sets of galleys. He had intercut in a thoughtful and, I thought, quite beautiful, way. I did not want to be hasty about it. I thanked him. I thought about it. A week later, I said I did not care to do it.

About that time, Condé Nast announced that it was going to revive *Vanity Fair.* The editor would be Richard Locke. Mr. Locke had been an editor at *The New York Times Book Review.* He had, as it happened, been the editor of my review of the Woodward and Armstrong book. I thought I knew what would happen. Condé Nast would try to make *Vanity Fair* a literary success and a respected competitor with *The New Yorker.* In about five years, they would discover it was not that easy. In five years, Mr. Shawn would be truly old, and faltering. Both magazines would be in trouble. Condé Nast would buy *The New Yorker* and merge it with *Vanity Fair.* Richard Locke would be boss of the merged publication. I discussed this with friends. There certainly did not seem to be a place for me at *The New Yorker.* I asked Luis Sanjurjo, a former Civil Rights attorney and a dear friend, whether he thought I ought to go to *Vanity Fair.* He said he did. I asked whether I ought to take "Orcas Island." He said yes. I asked whether he would help me. He said he would.

I had lunch with Mr. Locke. Luis devised an arrangement whereby I would work, two days a week, as the magazine's only consulting editor and be paid quite a lot. Mr. Locke bought "Orcas Island," agreed to publish it, unchanged and under a pseudonym, in his first or second issue; and to buy other fiction by me, under contracts—which, as it happened, I did not sign. I went to see Mr. Shawn. "They will publish 'Orcas Island'?" he said. "Unchanged, under a pseudonym, the way you wanted it?" I said, "Yes." He said he regretted what had happened. Before I signed any contract with *Vanity Fair* for other fiction, however, he would like to look at any other pieces—scraps, completed stories, whatever I had been working on. "I might have another idea," he said. This may be an odd place to say that I loved him. I did love him. I took out my notebooks and turned a lot of pages—not all of them, but a lot—over to him.

Three days later, I was in Washington. I found a message from Mr. Shawn on my answering machine. I called him. He was in a rage. "What is this material?" he said. "I have never seen it before." I said it was scraps, stories, whatever, that he had asked me to show him, before I showed anything further to *Vanity Fair*. "I don't understand what it has to do with *Vanity Fair*," he said. "You said you had given them 'Orcas Island.' That story was accepted here. That story was edited here. This other material, these pages, were accepted here. I have to be candid. This is breach of contract." I could not think of anything to say.

Back in New York, I took my belongings—my books, bulletin board, curtains, files—out of my office. I went to see the *New Yorker*'s lawyer, Milton Greenstein. I told him what had happened. "Shawn used those words? He said breach of contract?" Mr. Greenstein asked. I said, Yes. I started to tell him all the other things I was concerned about. He said, "I've got it. I'll handle it. Don't worry." Within hours, Mr. Shawn called me in, to discuss some ideas he had for *Vanity Fair.* He seemed genuinely to wish them well.

Mr. Locke seemed enthusiastic about ideas I brought to him. I worked very hard. I could not help noticing that although Mr. Locke treated me with the utmost respect and kindness, nothing I said seemed to have any effect. Alex Liberman began to take me to lunch. The magazine, it was becoming clear, was about to be godawful. I resigned before the first issue was published. Before I left, I persuaded the magazine to buy one story by Saul Bellow, one by Donald Barthelme, one by Frank Conroy, and one by Deborah Eisenberg, Wally Shawn's fiancée—an immensely talented writer, all of whose stories, until then, had been rejected by *The New Yorker.* Throughout this period, Mr. Shawn regularly called me in to discuss his suggestions for *Vanity Fair.*

Chapter Five

My timing was off about Condé Nast; and Richard Locke did not make it. I was not absolutely wrong. The end, after all, is not quite yet. In 1984, Advance Publications bought a minority interest in *The New Yorker.* Si Newhouse said, as people do say when they are planning takeovers, that he had no interest in acquiring a larger stake in the magazine, that he wanted only to share, along with the present owners, in its future. Several of us, including Jane Kramer and Michael Arlen, had gone to see Mr. Shawn, over the years, to ask whether he and the Fleischmanns had taken any steps to insulate the magazine from being taken over. It had been rumored, in the early sixties, that the Newhouses had considered buying *The New Yorker.* The magazine's owners had been so spooked that they immediately shifted their printing operation from Condé Nast, in Stamford, Connecticut, where layouts had gone by train, or even by courier (Brendan Gill used to say, in saddlebags)—to Donnelly, in Chicago, where texts were beamed electronically. Donnelly printed both *Time* and

Newsweek. For newsmagazines, which often needed to update, or otherwise change their covers at the last minute, this technology made sense. For *The New Yorker,* with its timeless or at least non-topical artists' covers, and its virtually scoop-free copy, the technology made no sense at all. The magazine, by a fluke of its management, was almost incredibly rich in cash. When Mr. Arlen and Ms. Kramer raised the takeover question, however, Mr. Shawn was not spooked. He spoke to them with that combination of innocence and knowingness that made people reluctant ever to raise such questions with him twice.

When Advance Publications bought its first shares, I asked a friend, Samuel Reed, then the editor of *American Heritage,* whether he could think of anyone who might buy the magazine and leave it with Mr. Shawn until he died or was ready to retire. Mr. Reed said I ought to try George Weidenfeld, that he might persuade Ann Getty. "Or you could try Sid Bass." I called George Weidenfeld. "I want them to start small," he said. "I just want them to get their feet wet. I don't want them to begin by antagonizing the Newhouses." Later, he said he had in fact checked; it was already too late. I called Sid Bass. He said he would look into it and think about it. He called back. "I think I would lose my shirt," he said.

Mr. Shawn, meanwhile, had suggested I write a column, about trials. "There are only two kinds of stories that are innately interesting," he said. "Games, and trials. Even if you know the outcome, they are always full of suspense." I had never thought of that. I said I was worried, though, that trials were long, and courtrooms were confining and oppressive. "All right. You don't *have* to do it," he said. Within the week, at a birthday party, I saw Tony Sifton. He had, by then, become a federal judge. I told him about the conversation with Mr. Shawn. Tony said, "Courtrooms are not at all confining. The average federal trial lasts less than fifteen days." I went back to Mr. Shawn. I said I would be glad to have a trials column. I asked whether I might construe trials as broadly or as narrowly as I liked—divorce proceedings, say, or trials by ordeal, or in Saudi Arabia. He said that would be fine.

At a dinner party, given by Jesse Kornbluth and Katherine Johnson, I was seated next to Donald Marron, head of Paine Webber. My second novel, *Pitch Dark,* had by then been published. Mr. Kornbluth had written a long, friendly piece in *New York Magazine.* Mr. Marron had read in that piece that I worked at *The New Yorker.* He said that he had been buying more shares, in secret, on behalf of Mr. Newhouse, and that he and Si had great plans for the magazine, especially in an age of television. I left the table, to call Mr. Shawn at home. I had noticed, over the years, that Mr. Shawn rather liked a bit of gossip. He received this new information with a kind of chortling interest, as though it were gossip of any other kind. I had lunch, at Pearl's, with Felix Rohatyn, whom I had met through Jimmy Lipton, a poet and writer of soap operas, who rented the floor above me in the brownstone where I lived. I asked Mr. Rohatyn whether he would talk to Mr. Shawn about arranging, if necessary, a takeover that would protect Mr. Shawn's editorship. He said he would be glad to. I went to Mr. Shawn and asked whether he would like to talk to Felix Rohatyn. He said he would. They met and talked. Mr. Rohatyn said that Mr. Shawn had reacted like any ordinary chief executive of a company that is subject to takeover—incredulous, intractable, unwilling to cede control even to the degree that would be required in order to find a friendly buyer and resume control.

"Mr. Newhouse says he has no interest in buying the magazine," Mr. Shawn said to each of us who asked. "I have to take him at his word."

By the time Advance Publications bought the rest of *The New Yorker,* Mr. Shawn appeared positively serene. He, and Ms. Ross, had begun to demonize the Fleischmanns. Ms. Ross says, in her book, that Warren Buffett had called and told Mr. Shawn he would like to buy *The New Yorker,* and turn it over to Mr. Shawn; that Mr. Shawn had asked him whether he would be willing to preserve the position of Peter Fleischmann; that Mr. Buffett said no; and that Mr. Shawn therefore, out of loyalty to Mr. Fleischmann, turned him down. The story is obviously, in all its many facets, silly. Mr. Fleischmann was the owner. There was no way Mr. Buffett could have bought the magazine and preserved the position of the previous owner, since Mr. Buffett himself would be the owner. If Mr. Shawn, moreover, had really acted out of loyalty to Mr. Fleischmann, that loyalty—and indeed every other practical and moral consideration—would have required him to call Mr. Fleischmann and convey Mr. Buffett's offer to him. Mr. Shawn had begun to invite to his office what he called "the Committee," a group of writers and other staff members, to discuss the takeover and its terms. The group, which I came to think of as the Committee of Loons, seemed to believe it had certain powers, of definition and of decision about what would happen next.

To contrast his loyalty to Mr. Fleischmann's treachery, Mr. Shawn kept saying, "The irony is that I was about to pick up the phone to call a Benefactor," when Mr. Fleischmann had assured him that the magazine was his to run. And he was "again about to call this Benefactor" when he received word that Mr. Newhouse had bought the magazine. This "Benefactor" may have been Mr. Buffett, or even Mr. Rohatyn, or someone else, or an allegorical figure, or no one. But Mr. Shawn was now sanguine, certain of his ability to guide and teach Mr. Newhouse. Mr. Newhouse had said he would leave everything about the magazine unchanged—would in fact be honored to leave it unchanged—and "I have no reason not to take him at his word." The Committee members, meanwhile, said that the magazine was caught in a classic "bear hug," this friendly but unwelcome and coercive takeover, and that the staff's response should be "scorched earth" if Mr. Newhouse refused to accept the terms the Committee would impose. This is where the loon factor seemed to come in. One writer said he had a friend, "an attorney," who must remain anonymous and "advise us clandestinely, because of his own position at his law firm." This person said there was a new sort of "provision or contract we could try out," which would impose on Mr. Newhouse certain obligations to the staff. This person would draw up—presumably clandestinely and anonymously, although it was hard to see why his name would have jeopardized his position at his law firm—this document, which Mr. Newhouse, for some equally unfathomable reason, would sign. At one point, Ms. Ross turned to me. "Renata, you're a friend of the Newhouses," she said. "You see all those people, socially. You say you went to college with Mrs. Newhouse. You wrote for *Vanity Fair*. Why don't you tell us what they're like." I said, "I did go to college with Mrs. Newhouse. She is my friend." Later, Jane Kramer said to me, "You were sandbagged." I felt I was. Gradually, over a few weeks, the Committee disbanded. Everyone went back to work.

Mr. Shawn and Mr. Newhouse seemed to hit it off. Ms. Ross became sunny-natured, as she had not been in years, and seemed to think that she and Mr. Shawn had at last found an ally in battles and antagonisms that went back for years—against Mr. Botsford, Ms. Malcolm, Mr. Angell, Mr. Greenstein, the advertising department, the fiction department, all the many people by whom she thought Mr. Shawn had been misunderstood, betrayed, and thwarted all these years. Mr. Newhouse, she said, supported Mr. Shawn as the Fleischmanns never had. In a speech, Mr. Newhouse had said that three men had profoundly influenced him: his own father, Alexander Liberman, and William Shawn. He was accepting Mr. Shawn's advice even about advertising. This view seemed to me curious. Almost all members of the old advertising department had been fired. The new advertising staff had been hired, and was run, by the new publisher, Steven Florio.

Mr. Florio had been brought in from *Gentleman's Quarterly.* He was young, blustering, cheerful, coarse, incompetent. In his first interviews, he said, "Everyone is waiting for Steve Florio to fall on his ass." No one, so far as one knew, was waiting for anything of the kind. My favorite utterance of Mr. Florio's occurred years later, when Tina Brown became editor of *The New Yorker. The New York Times* ran a piece about the transition. Mr. Florio was quoted in the piece. He said that Mr. Shawn had once asked him, "Who is the best living editor?" It is hard to convey how unimaginable it was that Mr. Shawn should pose such a question to anyone, let alone to Steven Florio.

"Tina Brown," Mr. Florio said he had replied, "because she has her ear to the ground and hears the rumbles."

Mr. Shawn, according to Mr. Florio, had responded, "I make the rumbles." The line, needless to say, even the thought, is inconceivable on the part of Mr. Shawn.

The *Times,* as I say, quoted this. No one but Mr. Florio could have dreamed up this whole exchange. It was purely (certainly not the right word) Florio.

This is not to say that, before Florio, the *New Yorker*'s advertising department was above reproach. Several times, driving my car from Connecticut to New York, with the radio tuned to an all-news station, I heard what I thought was peculiarly irritating static, which disappeared when I switched to another AM station and recurred when I switched back.

"This full minute of bird calls," an incredibly creepy voice, which might have belonged to an overbred child molester, said, "has been brought to you by *The New Yorker.* Yes. *The New Yorker.*"

After I had heard it a third time, I called Pete Spellman, an old friend in the advertising department. In the most gingerly way, I asked him about the commercial. It turned out he had worked on it and was extremely proud of it. The bird calls, he said, were soothing. The voice, not a child molester's at all, was very effective and highly regarded. A mistake, I thought. His or mine. But Pete Spellman was gone. What remained was Florio. Ms. Ross said that, now that they had seen one Florio, she and Mr. Shawn were beginning to see Florios everywhere: his bluster, his look. He had given Mr. Shawn a color television set. Ms. Ross said Mr. Shawn had always avoided color sets, believing the radiation might cause cancer. She was not sure whether or not he had turned the new set on. Several things were clear to most of us about Mr. Florio: He might be amusing to Mr. Shawn. He did not understand *The New Yorker.* He was not going to be much good at bringing advertising to the magazine.

For some months in 1983, it seemed plausible that Chip

McGrath, alone, would become Mr. Shawn's successor. He had the support of Roger Angell. Mr. Shawn, and even Mr. Newhouse, for all one knew, had chosen him as well. Fairly soon, it became evident that they had not chosen him. I once asked Mr. McGrath how he felt about this period. "I've had the ego ground out of me for so many years," he said. "I guess I feel the same way about it as everybody else." Mr. McGrath told Luis Sanjurjo that he was withdrawing his name from contention and going off to write. Months after that, Richard Avedon called me. "Chip says he won't believe Mr. Shawn is actually leaving until he hears it from Frank E. Campbell." "Who is Frank E. Campbell?" I asked, thinking it must be some new person, perhaps from Condé Nast, working at the magazine. Avedon laughed. "He meant the funeral home," he said.

In the early 1980s, there were two more *New Yorker* crises. One arose out of pieces by Janet Malcolm; the other from an article of my own. My own arose first. As part of my work for the Trials column, I had gone to many courtrooms: night court, family court, and so on. In 1995, at the federal courthouse in Manhattan, two libel trials were running simultaneously. One was the suit of General William C. Westmoreland against CBS, for having accused him, among other things, of having falsified statistics about deaths in Vietnam. The other was by the Israeli general Ariel Sharon against *Time,* for having accused him of having condoned, and even encouraged, the massacre of Lebanese in refugee camps at Sabra and Shatilla. Both accusations appeared in reporting pieces, which purported to be scoops, and claimed to have solid, heretofore secret, supporting documentation. Both defendants—the network and the news magazine—were represented by the same law firm: Cravath, Swaine & Moore. Both stories turned out to be false, although the high standard set, in libel law, for proving "actual malice" made what were, in effect, victories for the plaintiffs less than absolute. I covered the trials. I also studied what reporters, with breaking stories and frequent deadlines, could not possibly have time for: the depositions in the cases.

One day, near the end of the Sharon trial, I had a setback that set clear limits on any idea I had of the cachet of press credentials, let alone *New Yorker* credentials, even within the city of New York. I was dressed for court—in heels, a suit, gloves. I had more than two hundred dollars in my purse. I wondered whether to take a taxi or the subway to Foley Square. A verdict was due. The subway was faster. I went down the stairs to the subway station, at Lexington and Seventy-seventh, bought five tokens, put one in the turnstile, and passed through. A moment later, I noticed a large newsstand. I wished I had bought the papers. I wondered whether it was worth going out through the turnstile again, buying a paper, and wasting another token to come back in. I had been prepared, after all, to take a taxi; the price of an extra token seemed negligible. I went out, I thought, to the newsstand, bought the papers, came back to the turnstile, and prepared to put my token in the slot. I dropped the token on the ground. A young lady, in jeans and a tee shirt, approached, picked up my token, and handed it to me. She looked as though she were about to ask me something. I smiled. She took my wrist and put handcuffs on it. I looked around. A small band of people, handcuffed to one another, stood behind the turnstiles, near a swinging door, which had been lashed into an open position. Someone came in through that door. She put handcuffs on him. "This is a sweep," she said. "But I was about to pay," I said. I held out my token. "I was on my way in." "You are in," she said.

It turned out that I had never gone out. The newsstand was inside the turnstiles, and I had been inside the whole time. I had never left. There was something so peculiar, however, about my fumbling with a token—impervious to but in plain sight of a group in handcuffs—the young lady felt she had to arrest me. Anyway, she needed to fill a quota of fifteen arrests to complete her assignment. I showed her my press card, my *New Yorker* identification. She called her partner over, then handcuffed me to a young black woman who was already part of the group. "We'll straighten it out when we get to the academy," she said. "I'll tell them it was a misunderstanding. You was confused."

"You weren't confused," said my new best friend, to whom I was handcuffed. "I watched the whole thing. You were dis*or*iented." Our group was standing near a pay phone. I said I would like to call my lawyer. The transit officers didn't even look around. Two men in the group, evidently with some experience, said we had a right to be moved to a holding pen beneath Grand Central. There was a lot of back and forth between these men and the transit officers. "Fuck you." "Fuck *you.*" And so on. We were each allowed to make one phone call. I called Gardner Botsford. He said he would find out where the police academy was, and meet me there. In due course, we were loaded onto a bus, which took us to the academy.

Mr. Botsford was already there. I rushed over to embrace him—inadvertently dragging along my new best friend. He said he had spoken to the people upstairs. Everything was taken care of. He left. When our group got upstairs, we were searched. "This is the one," an officer said. "She's got the four tokens, and two hundred dollars." They took us into an assembly hall, where we were seated, and handcuffed to the people on either side. The doors were guarded by officers with German shepherds. They found several felons, and parole violators, especially among the messengers in our group. I was released early—not in time for the court's morning session (there was no verdict), but in time for a lunch date with Bayard Rustin. He said he would be more meticulous, in view of my experience, with the use of his transit pass.

I wrote my Trials piece. Mr. Shawn published it. *Time,* CBS, Cravath, and many others, particularly media people, were outraged. Mr. Shawn, *The New Yorker* and I were sued for libel. The plaintiff, a young man named Greg Rushford, had not been a major figure in the trials, or in my piece. I had quoted something the judge said about him. In the event, the court dismissed the suit—finding that there could have been no libel, for at least two reasons: The quote was accurate. Even if it had not been accurate, it was not defamatory. A sign of where most of the press stood in this matter was a piece by Eleanor Randolph, at that time a reporter for *The Washington Post.* The suit had been dismissed, she said, on the grounds that the quote was "mere opinion." In the meantime, we discovered that Mr. Rushford had been a recent employee of the fugitive Robert Vesco, and there was reason to think he had not really been suing on his own behalf. My apartment, too, had been expertly burgled; the only items removed had been my answering machine, a word processor (which I did not yet know how to use), a memory typewriter, and some files. The *New Yorker*'s lawyers, and mine, in the case, Leonard Garment, and Rosalyn Mazer, said I could not mention either the burglary or the Vesco connection until the case was over. The piece, called "Reckless Disregard," was published in book form, but *The New Yorker* and I took a lot of flak for it. Had I known what a lot of consternation the piece would cause, I would either not have written it, or been more vehement in my own view of the conduct of the media defendants in both trials.

Ms. Malcolm had a harder time. She had written a piece about Jeffrey Masson, a complicated figure who had once been appointed head of the Freud Archive and then had turned on Freud—accusing him, among other things, of dismissing as fantasy what he knew to be widespread and genuine cases of child abuse, in order to maintain the popularity of his theories. Anyone who read the piece would know that Ms. Malcolm, whose own father was an analyst, disagreed with Masson. On the other hand, the fairness of her report was such that I, for example, was persuaded by Masson, as she represented his views. The portrayals of people in the piece, moreover, had such accuracy and vitality, that the characters seemed to spring to life right after the piece was published. Mr. Masson, who had sued someone, in the piece, and received a generous settlement, came to life—and sued Ms. Malcolm and *The New Yorker.* Then, Ms. Malcolm published another piece, "The Journalist and the Murderer." It began with the line

> Every journalist who is not too stupid or too full of himself to notice what is going on knows that what he does is morally indefensible.

Ms. Malcolm went on to say that all journalists play upon the vanity of their subjects, enlist their trust and then betray them. It could be argued that an editor, foreseeing what would happen, might have urged Ms. Malcolm to cut or modify these lines. She did not need them. Many reporters, especially in the era of celebrity journalism, far from betraying the subjects in their pieces, praise them and cater rather slavishly to them—so that the reporter's fortunes and his subject's rise together. On the other hand, "All happy families are alike" is not entirely true, either. Tolstoy was never vilified for it. Ms. Malcolm made several reporters look really bad. The major figure in her piece was Joe McGinniss, who had written a book about Jeffrey MacDonald, a doctor in prison for the murder of his family. MacDonald proclaimed his innocence. McGinniss led him to believe that McGinniss believed in it too—then portrayed him as guilty. The doctor, from his prison, had sued the journalist. Other journalists, who were called as witnesses in Mr. McGinniss's defense, looked foolish and venal. Ms. Malcolm's piece created such a storm of anger and vilification that it affected the outcome of her trial in the Jeffrey Masson libel case.

Journalists would now cross a crowded room to tell one how offended they had been by Ms. Malcolm's slight on their profession. The publishing correspondent of a major newspaper told me, for example, that he felt hurt, insulted, and embarrassed by her words. I could not understand it. It seemed to me that reporters who did not behave in the way Ms. Malcolm was describing had only to realize that they were not included in her remarks, and that was that. Mr. Masson, however, was surely emboldened by the reception of Ms. Malcolm's piece. In the suit as he originally filed it, he had listed many quotations attributed to him as words he had never spoken. It turned out that the vast majority of these quotations had actually been recorded by Ms. Malcolm, when she taped their interviews. In the process of legal discovery, however, Mr. Masson received the complete transcripts of Ms. Malcolm's tapes. He found five other quotations, which did not appear in the transcripts, characterized those as libelous, and revised his suit. Ms. Malcolm said that even these quotes were from her notes of their conversations. Many reporters, after all, do not use tape recorders, but rely entirely on their notes. She could not find the notebook in question, however, at the time. Years later, she did find it, along with evidence that could leave no doubt of its authenticity. But by then the trial—trials, rather (the first trial ended in a hung jury, Ms. Malcolm won the second)—were over. Ms. Malcolm's long ordeal had included intense, hostile coverage of the case. Her pieces, her demeanor, her style of dress had been the subject of unfriendly reporting. Even her speech had been routinely and groundlessly described as foreign, Czech. Ms. Malcolm's parents were, in fact, refugees from Czechoslovakia. There was not a trace of an accent in her speech. By the time the case was over, opinion had turned. Ms. Malcolm's views were widely accepted, and her pieces were cited as classics. But it took six years. Photographers don't like to be photographed. Surgeons require nearly twice the amount of anesthesia ordinary patients require to undergo surgery. Journalists are the least receptive to professional scrutiny by their colleagues. They react, sometimes unconsciously, sometimes with the utmost deliberation, to avenge themselves.

At what appeared to be a serene time in Mr. Shawn's relations with Si Newhouse, I happened to be on a plane with Si, returning from Palm Beach. We sat together for a time, talking about the magazine. He was full of admiration for Mr. Shawn, including a quality I had not considered: his skills as a "technician." In all the complexities of the man, and of the way he ran his publication, it had never occurred to me how swiftly, perfectly, decisively he dealt with the mechanics of putting out a weekly magazine—writers, artists, editors, proofs, checkers, the men in makeup, printers. There was no tension, and there were no mistakes. It was work he did with ease.

This was a period when no candidate for the succession was being considered. Mr. Newhouse, however, suddenly remarked on a related question—Mr. Shawn's lack of "a second man." I thought of friends who now struck me as belonging to this category: Michael Janeway at *The Atlantic Monthly,* under Robert Manning; James Chace at *Foreign Affairs,* under Hamilton Fish Armstrong. They were indispensable to their editors-in-chief. In almost every respect, they ran their publications. But year after year, they were passed over for the editorship, until it became obvious they were never going to have it—for reasons that had always seemed to me inexplicable. Now it became clear. The reasons had nothing to do with their respective talents. The explanation lay in the category and its definition: second man. If they were ever going to become chief of an enterprise, they had to leave the place where they were defined as second men. A "right-hand man" seems to be quite another matter. Right-hand men are indispensable to their bosses, but they work for a different sort of boss and are treated in a subtly different way. The boss is stronger. The right-hand man is an instrument of the boss's will, and paradoxically stronger for it. Second men exist in places where the boss tends to be weak, even a figurehead, without much confrontation or overt expression of the will. The exercise of will—whether it is the boss's, or the right-hand man's, or both—seems to be the decisive factor. Right-hand men do succeed their bosses. Shawn had been Ross's right-hand man.

Mr. Shawn, however, had neither—right-hand man, nor second man. What he did have was in a related category: office wife. Many executives seem to have office wives, in the form of secretaries or subordinate colleagues: women on whom they rely, and with whom they consult throughout the office day. This is by no means always, or even very often, a sexual matter. Rosemary Woods was probably President Nixon's office wife. Robert Gottlieb, the editor at Knopf, had an office wife: Martha Kaplan. Ms. Kaplan was devoted to her boss, and trusted by him. When they shared an interest, they even traveled together. But Ms. Kaplan's friendship with Mr. Gottlieb was such that its source was work. Ms. Kaplan dealt, on Mr. Gottlieb's behalf, with writers and editors alike as a consummate professional, bright, steady, funny, and extraordinarily attuned to the moods of the people she was dealing with.

Mr. Shawn's office wife, for many years, was Lillian Ross. He went to her office several times a day. They often went to restaurants, plays, and concerts in the evening. Ms. Ross says theirs was a forty-year love affair. She clearly exercised immense influence over him. She did not deal with other people on his behalf, however. She seemed, rather, to describe and represent other people to him, in the way she saw them. There was a lot of fear and envy of Ms. Ross at the magazine. After the stories that comprise her novel, *Vertical and Horizontal,* were published, the fiction editors routinely turned down all stories by her which fell within their jurisdiction. Mr. Shawn both saw this and did not see it. "The fiction department is the only part of the magazine that is political," he said, clearly meaning office politics. On another occasion, he spoke of the fiction editors' "suspicious unanimity." The only other department with the power to accept or reject pieces was the art department, but it had no bureaucracy and no role in office politics. "The art department is perfect," Mr. Shawn said. He also both saw and did not see the increasing bitterness and suspicion with which Ms. Ross seemed to regard other members of the staff. It was part of his nature to humor everyone. It was one of his strengths. But humoring everyone, on all sides of a question, while it may avoid unpleasant confrontation, is also certain to result in the strain of holding several sharply divergent, mutually incompatible views. That was increasingly Mr. Shawn's situation. Ms. Ross was persistent. With time, the suspiciousness that seems, in any case, to be a concomitant of aging—added to a quite genuine distrust of others in the ongoing succession crises, and magnified further by Ms. Ross's views—seemed to color and undermine Mr. Shawn's own intuitions about people.

Not infrequently, yet another category, never as reliable as the other three, appears to supplant the office wife—the protégé. In Mr. Shawn's case, Jonathan Schell, in Mr. Gottlieb's, Adam Gopnik, were protégés. Protégés do not linger. Though they may rivet the boss's attention, they tend to act upon their agendas and move on. An office wife, unlike a second man or even a right-hand man, seems to offer no real protection from the world. After my conversation with Mr. Newhouse, with no plausible successor, I said to Mr. Shawn, "You know, if you ever do retire, there's going to be a scramble."

"There isn't going to be any scramble," he replied.

In all the years of *The New Yorker*'s existence, one sort of editing seems to have been lacking: editing, in the broadest sense, for meaning, for implications, for what, for one reason or another is implied by what you are saying, or what it is simply not all right to say. There was, in that sense, no governing intelligence. This could be a matter of almost silly detail. Edith Oliver, for example, when she reviewed theater Off-Broadway, wrote of a play by Racine, performed abridged and in English translation, "I have not read the original, but . . ." There was no reason to go beyond that "but." A checker, once reading a poem by Ogden Nash, which began "Today I am thirty," had noted Mr. Nash's birthdate in the margin, and added, "He is thirty-one." With the same degree of attention, someone ought to have written in the margin of Ms. Oliver's piece, "Why not? Go and read it then. Or at least spare the reader the confession that you have not done what he has every right to expect a professional critic to do." Ms. Oliver, and other reviewers, would sometimes write that a play or a performance was "full of sound and fury, signifying nothing." Apart from their staleness, these are not words that it is permissible for a critic to use. The comment, no matter what the subject, is empty and wrong.

More broadly, for all the attention to detail, there was no one to say that a writer's reasoning, for example, had a crucial flaw in it, or that his facts did not bear out his argument, or even that he seemed unaware of what he actually said. A profile, by John Newhouse, of King Hussein of Jordan, described him, without question or reservation, as "a descendant of Mohammed." No one, from checking on up, seemed to remark that the magazine appeared thereby to endorse, and convey as factual, a belief held only by a tiny, isolated faction of Islam. The lack of a governing intelligence has persisted to the present day. A recent, widely-read piece about the relative influence of various factors upon the development of children was almost a model of logical incoherence, questionable research, and debatable fact. The piece presented as "a new idea" the notion that children are powerfully affected by peers, then presented as an argument for the relative unimportance of parents what turned out to be a slim claim, not even for peers but for heredity.

And though they were, in *The New Yorker,* so infrequent that discovering them could become a source of pleasure, there were occasional editing lapses. A few sentences, for example, in another piece by John Newhouse, declared, rather more than once, and more than really meticulous editing might permit, something beyond dispute. The piece was a profile of Lord Carrington, the British diplomat. It said he was English.

> Everyone agrees that Carrington is very English. Although he knows the world well and gets along with foreigners of every kind, he isn't especially cosmopolitan. "He doesn't dislike foreigners—it's just that he doesn't really like them," a friend says. "Peter is very English, and happiest in the company of other Englishmen." The net impression is that Carrington is not insular but is quintessentially English, and . . .

A few columns further down, on another subject:

> Henry Kissinger has a conceptual mind, and in his public utterances, whether or not they were made when he was in or out of office, he has often cited the need for a conceptual framework in which to develop policy.

Mr. Newhouse was not well served in the editing of this piece. In both passages, one knows, certainly, what he is getting at. But somewhere in the margins, there should have been a note that Lord Carrington's nationality was never in much doubt. There should have been a query about what constitutes a conceptual, or for that matter, a non-conceptual mind. "Whether or not they were made when he was in or out of office," however, is almost absolutely incomprehensible. "Whether or not inside" is a possible construction. "Whether or not outside" is another. "Whether inside or outside" is a third. "Whether or not inside or outside" does not make sense.

Some pieces, of course, are extremely careful, thoughtful, written in full consciousness of what it is new and permissible to say, and what has been said already, while other writing—perhaps better, through being relatively fluent and spontaneous—is not. Very early in my years at *The New Yorker,* as I was trying to write criticism, I said to Harold Rosenberg that if I thought hard enough about the opening sentence of a piece, what could be said for and against it, what had already been said on the subject and so on, I wound up with a truism. The sentenced vanished, and the piece with it.

"Oh, yes," he said, "It happens to me all the time. It is like Charlie Brown. You back up so far for the kickoff that by the time you have run up and reached the ball, it's gone."

Mr. Rosenberg was so painstaking in the depth at which he wrote—as was Joe Mitchell, at the opposite extreme of hard-won lightness—that he did not need editing, except for the sort of mistakes all writers tend to make and overlook. There were also very talented writers with idiosyncracies, technical strengths, quirks, and failings, which the best *New Yorker* editors had special skills and patience to accommodate. One writer might have a strong sense of structure and a gift for anecdote, but no gift at all for research, fact, or detail. The symbol, in a manuscript or a galley, for a fact the writer means to include but does not yet know is (tk), for To Come. The writer might submit copy that reads:

> On August (tk), 19(tk), as the invasion swept the beaches of (tk), France, Conrad (tk) Emse waited with his stiletto in a dark corner of the (tk) Imperial Palace outside (tk) for the last member of the (tk) choir to come in.

The whole mechanism of *The New Yorker,* from checking and copy-editing upward, could deal with just this sort of piece.

Another kind of writer would have pages, thousands of pages, with masses of facts and details—without sequence or structure. An editor would take a fragment of a sentence from page 290, connect it to another from page 42, take up a set of facts from pages 9 through 16, and compose an opening sentence. He might proceed that way through an entire manuscript, stitching pieces of the mass into a cohesive whole. There was no editor better at this than Bill Whitworth.

A third kind of writer might just require judicious, in fact, perfect cutting, to remove what is extraneous, to reveal a well-formed piece. For this kind of writer, most writers, there was no better editor than Gardner Botsford. He cut for clarity, humor, form. A vexed question at *The New*

Yorker, through all the years of Ross and Shawn, was obscenity. By the sixties, everyone was using obscenities of all kinds. The strongest Anglo-Saxon words in the language were so common that their power was nearly gone. Still, Mr. Shawn, in his words, "held the line." The first use of "shit" occurred in a piece by Anthony Lewis, in a quotation of President Nixon from a transcript of the White House tapes. Mr. Shawn went on, in my view like Horton the elephant, nurturing, amid all the pressures and distractions, the egg of civil discourse, or whatever he thought it was. Nothing came of it, I think, except perhaps the touching spectacle of faithfulness itself. Meanwhile, people tried to sneak things by. In an early piece, I quoted Rick Sklar, the director of a pop music radio station, to the effect that a new recording "is going to be a mother." The piece went as far as page proofs. Mr. Shawn called me in. "Galley twelve, line eight," he began. "The word 'mother,' the question has been raised . . ." "It means," I said, "that this recording will give rise to several little records like it. If we can't use the word 'mother' in the magazine . . ."

"All right," Mr. Shawn said. "But would you just check it again with Mr. Sklar?"

I called Rick Sklar. He hesitated. Then he said, "All right. It's fine. Put 'motherfucker' back in." I said, "No, no." The word "mother" ran.

By the time of Pauline Kael, there were so many end runs around the standard—double entendres, phrases and sentences of the utmost coarseness—that Mr. Shawn's position seemed quite forlorn. George Roy Hill, the film director, was a cousin of John Doar's. They both came from a very small town, New Richmond, Wisconsin. One evening, in the late seventies, Mr. Hill, his wife, Mr. Doar, and I were having dinner. Mr. Hill said that he had gone to great lengths, and incurred high expenses for the studio, in using genuine outdoor sounds for his movie. Ms. Kael, who disliked all his films, had written, with bitter scorn, that he had not troubled with the authentic, but had used canned sounds.

"Why that's awful," I said. "You should have asked for a correction."

"I did," he said. I asked what had happened. "Nothing," he said. Whom had he written to? "Pauline." The wrong person, I thought. He should have written to the editor. "What did you say?" I asked. "I don't remember," he said. "It started out, 'You cunt.' " I saw there was nothing to be done.

It is only in the years since Mr. Shawn, however, that it has become clear that, once he had stood by his standard on obscenity for so long, there was hardly any turning back. Rough speech in *The New Yorker* still seems so alien that it leaps off the page—not powerfully, however, and not purely, but most often dully, as a shattering of something already in smithereens.

Chapter Six

Adam Gopnik had come to Knopf after a time as features editor, under Art Cooper, at the monthly Condé Nast publication, *GQ*. A frail, diminutive man in his mid-thirties, he had dark hair in a little-boy haircut, his bangs, more like a fringe, cut long and straight down across the forehead almost to the eyebrows. From time to time, in a little periodic mannerism, he would jut out his chin and his lower lip and, blowing upward, exhale a little puff of air, which would lift that fringe, and let it drop again. He walked stoop-shouldered. His coloring was high, a reddening of the cheeks, sometimes with outright blushes. Often, he would punctuate his rushed, already staccato delivery of words (sentences, apologies, disclaimers, reiterations of the name of the person he was talking to) with a little, nervous, mirthless, self-deprecating laugh, *eh, eh, eh, eh, eh,* always five beats, five *eh*s, like little dry intervals of machine gun fire, interruptions of himself. This laugh, which required only the slightest opening of the mouth and not even the semblance of a smile, seemed designed as a form of charm, boyishness, humility, with which he tried to moderate the impact of what he apparently regarded as the brilliance of his conversation, a strange alternating current of flattery and self-promotion, accompanied by rapid, in fact incessant, blinking, and the little upward puffs of air.

When I met Adam Gopnik, he was thirty. He had called Richard Avedon, asking to interview him for a piece in *GQ*. In a short time, they became friends. The piece for *GQ* was no longer mentioned. Avedon, an old friend, with whom I had worked on a few projects, said that Adam reminded him of himself as a young man, excitable, ambitious, ideas striking him in the street, so that he had to stop at pay phones and call to express them to somebody. He and Adam, he said, might start a magazine. He brought Mr. Gopnik to Connecticut. We had dinner at a clam house in Westport. For the first hour or so, I thought there was going to be a magazine. Avedon certainly seemed to think so. Mr. Gopnik's idea, for the new magazine, seemed to be that they would publish Alice Munro. I think Alice Munro is one of the finest living writers of fiction, but she was not unpublished or unknown. Mr. Gopnik changed the subject. He and his wife, Martha, he said, were bringing a lawsuit against a ski resort. They had been sledding there, the sled had hit a rough patch with too little snow on it. His wife had hurt her back. I asked where she was now. Working on a movie, he said, but she had suffered, might never bear children, still had constant pain. A lawyer had taken their case, on a commission basis. In the event, Mr. Gopnik told me, they settled their suit at the last minute, for $90,000. When I congratulated him, he said, "Well, it's just enough to buy a word processor, and that's what we'll do." In time Mr. Gopnik and his wife, Martha Parker, became parents.

On Monday, January 12, 1987, at approximately four in the afternoon, I was in my house in Newtown, Connecticut, when Adam Gopnik called, from his office at Knopf. He wanted to discuss some concerns he had about his writing career. He was a protégé, by this time, both of Avedon and of Robert Gottlieb, but Kurt Varnedoe, director of the Museum of Modern Art and a mentor of Mr. Gopnik's before he came to Knopf, had called him to say that, although a recent piece by Mr. Gopnik was "a breakthrough" and "a star turn," some people might resent his brilliance as "showing off" and regard his humor as "clowning around on the page." The piece in question, about Krazy Kat, in *The New Republic,* was, I thought, unremarkable, but I had become accustomed to these calls, in which Mr. Gopnik would present, as criticism and in tones of concern, some extravagant compliment to himself. I commiserated. The doorbell rang. I had to hang up. A few minutes later, Mr. Gopnik called again. "This is just to tell you," he said, "Bob is the new editor of *The New Yorker,* effective in six weeks."

A few minutes later, Bill Honan, of *The New York Times,* called and asked me for a quote. I said I'd like to think about it. He said, "You've got about ten minutes." I thought about it. I came up with, "He was one of the greatest editors in the history of American letters. But I guess, if there had to be a successor, it should be Bob." I called to check it with Mr. Shawn. His line was busy. I called Bob Gottlieb. He said, "Do you want me to help you with your comment?" I said, "Not exactly. I was thinking I might say, 'He was one of the greatest editors in the history of American letters—' " Mr. Gottlieb said, "That's not true." I said, "After all these years, Bob. He is eighty." Mr. Gottlieb said, "Oh. You meant him."

I read him the full quote. He said, "I would be very grateful if you do that."

Bill Honan, an old friend from the days when he was chief of checking at *The New Yorker,* called again. His piece, with my quote in it, went to press. Many phone calls that night, to and from *New Yorker* people, and other friends. Adam Gopnik called again. He was worried. He had a story at *The New Yorker,* scheduled to run within the month. "Do you think they'll postpone it?" he said. "I know, it's not that important. It's just that that story means so much to me and Martha." Kurt Varnedoe, Mr. Gopnik also said, had told him that he must now seriously consider the possibility that he would have to choose between becoming Mr. Gottlieb's managing editor at *The New Yorker,* and being appointed his successor as Knopf's editor-in-chief.

The next morning, Tuesday, I took the train to Grand Central, and walked to the office. In the corridor of the nineteenth floor, I passed Daniel Menaker, one of the fiction editors. He looked extremely agitated. He did not say hello. I looked in at the office of Lee Lorenz, the art editor, with whom I was going to have lunch. A meeting of artists was going on in there. In my own office, the phone rang: Lillian Ross. I asked if she wanted to have a cup of coffee. She said she was working on a piece, but that she would drop in later. "Or you could drop in here," she said. "After all, you're in with management." She laughed. "On second thought, don't venture into the halls. Wait till Chip and Roger get hold of you. You and your big mouth. Couldn't you just say, 'No comment'?"

While I made and received phone calls, and waited for Lee Lorenz, a messenger knocked and delivered the rough copy of the magazine. The finished copy would be on the stands the next morning. What was remarkable about it, what remained remarkable about all the issues Mr. Shawn published between the announcement of his departure and the day of Bob's arrival, was the lack of a single important, valuable, or even moderately interesting piece. An editor other than Mr. Shawn, or perhaps just a man with better advice than he was apparently getting, would have shown in these issues just what he could do.

At lunch, in a Japanese restaurant, Lee said that the art people had been surprisingly calm for what he had expected. I said that, from the corridor, the meeting had looked turbulent. He said, No, that's only because it's Tuesday. Dan Menaker, he said, had brought news of a meeting of the whole staff scheduled for two o'clock that afternoon—although he had been careful to add that this was not his invitation, and that he did not know under whose auspices or on whose initiative it had been called. After lunch, I went to Lillian Ross's office. She was there with her poodle, Goldie. She said, "You look very well. I'm sorry I said that stuff about your big mouth." Then her tone changed. "You asked him about everything else, why didn't you discuss it with him? Or me? You've lost the respect of the people who love you here." I didn't respond. I just said, "Well, have we thought what the smart thing would be, or is it too late to be smart?" She said, "There's a meeting at two." I said, "I know."

"Why don't you come to it?" she said. "Explain what's so great about Bob Gottlieb. Why don't you come to the meeting, if you dare." I said I was planning to. She said, "That's very brave. And then you can explain to them what's so great about Bob Gottlieb, instead of telling it to the *Times*." I was used to this conversational style. I said, "Maybe I will, again maybe not, but let me decide it. Please don't direct questions at me." Ms. Ross said, "I won't ask you any questions. . . . The point is, the Newhouses had agreed to Chip." I said, mildly, "Obviously, they hadn't." I asked again whether she had any ideas. "I don't have any ideas," Ms. Ross said, in a scornful voice. "Why don't you say what you think?" I said I thought there were two different issues, and that it was crucial to keep them separate. One was whether Mr. Shawn could stay on. The other was whether he could choose his successor. "He's not going to be allowed to choose his successor. He has every right to stay on. It's his magazine. The staff doesn't care about the succession," I said. "They care about Mr. Shawn. But if he insists on choosing his successor, he'll be out, whether the staff supports him or not."

Ms. Ross smiled. "Let's wait and see," she said.

We set off, along the nineteenth-floor hallway, outside her office, toward the little staircase to the eighteenth floor. On the way, perhaps inadvertently but more probably out of anger, she speeded up to put distance between us. Gathered on the eighteenth floor, at the base of the stairs, near the shelves of disheveled daily newspapers, there were a few people in clusters. Mr. Shawn, eyeglasses in hand, stood more or less in their midst. A small crowd was gathering around him. The bare linoleum floor, the gray walls, the tall bookcases with locked glass doors and books that nobody ever used, books no one could remember who selected, left a small, unlikely space for a meeting. Harold Brodkey leaned against the shelves of newspapers. Daniel Menaker stood at a bend or angle in the staircase, where he could look upstairs or down, and where, so constricted was the architecture, he could actually lean his elbow, just above his head, on a section of the ceiling. I stood against one of those glass-paneled bookcases, among writers, editors, men from makeup. Mr. Shawn began to speak. He was too small to be seen or heard. People said, "Stand on the steps!" Lillian Ross relayed this suggestion to him. He had begun to have trouble with his hearing, and it became apparent that, under these circumstances, he could hardly hear at all.

It became like a film sequence. People kept trickling in along the eighteenth floor, or trooping, single file, down the stairs behind him, and it was touching then. Over where I was, to the right facing Mr. Shawn, were Bud Trillin, Henry Cooper, Bill McKibben, Jonathan Schell, Jim Lardner, and the rest of a motley group; to the left, Joseph Mitchell, Roger Angell, Ved Mehta, Janet Malcolm, whoever else—the fact was, none of us except the tallest could see all the rest. Mr. Shawn, eyeglasses in hand, climbed to about the third step, and began again. Still, people were filing down and trooping in. Mr. Shawn repeated what he had just said: "I heard about this spontaneous meeting. I have nothing prepared. I'm prepared to answer questions, if there are any."

A voice said, "Mr. Shawn, what happened?" Laughter. Mr. Shawn began one of those not quite accurate, or consistent, or for that matter entirely plausible accounts that some of us were used to by now. He and Chip had met only Monday morning (that is, yesterday, January 12, 1987), to confirm the succession. They had established that it would take place "some time this summer." The issue, in other words, became at once absurd, untenable—not the right of Mr. Shawn to stay, but the right to name his successor, and not even that. It had become a question of McGrath's right to take over "this summer," in other words, in about six months. Apart from the sheer implausibility of their having confirmed it just the day before, this utterly trivialized the matter. It was already clear that the Newhouses would not permit Mr. Shawn to name his successor. They had made it particularly clear that they did not accept Mr. McGrath. Since they were already giving Mr. Shawn six weeks (in other words, until March), that meant the entire fuss had been reduced to concern about a period from March to, say, July—an issue idiotic in itself. If this were really the issue, and if it had been properly or credibly drawn, there could be no doubt that the Newhouses would happily have permitted Mr. Shawn to stay on until July—or right through the summer if he liked.

Mr. Shawn said he had discussed all this with Mr. Newhouse when he last saw him, "six or eight weeks ago." But if this was true, why confirm it with Chip McGrath only yesterday morning? Mr. Shawn said he must remind people, "in all fairness," that at the time of the "contract with the editorial staff" (this was a vague letter of agreement, which Mr. Newhouse had eventually signed to allay the anxieties of the Committee of Loons), Mr. Newhouse had not relinquished the right to name a successor "although the committee fought very hard for it." "Anyway," he said, "that contract had no legal meaning."

"But it was a breach!" someone called out. "In that contract Newhouse did promise to consult, before naming a successor, with the editorial staff."

"In all fairness," Mr. Shawn said, "I think Mr. Newhouse has forgotten all about that contract."

Gardner Botsford had telephoned Mr. Shawn, the night before, to express sympathy and to ask whether Mr. Shawn had had any hint that this was going to happen. Mr. Shawn had said, "No. It was a bombshell." He now told the staff it came as a complete surprise—that, in fact, he had thought

Newhouse was just coming by to keep abreast of the succession. Suddenly, Mr. Shawn said he could see how Newhouse might have thought he had set March 10 for his retirement, but that was a mistake. Passing right over this curious discrepancy, a complete surprise, a bombshell, an understandable mistake based on a date he might have set, Mr. Shawn said that Mr. Newhouse had given two reasons why McGrath would not be a suitable successor. The first reason was that he might be too respectful of *The New Yorker*'s traditions. (Laughter.) The second was that he might, on the contrary, be too radical. (Laughter.)

The question now, Mr. Shawn said, was "What, if anything, do we do to keep *The New Yorker* what it is?"

A voice, from makeup, I think (as the meeting grew and moved about, it became ever harder to see, or to recognize by voice, just who was speaking), said, "Maybe the answer is for each of us to keep right on doing what we have been doing."

That, of course, was not the answer on the agenda, was in fact the last answer Mr. Shawn and the group assembled really had in mind. Someone suggested walking out, but that was ignored as well. Tom Whiteside, a particularly slow-talking writer, said he had felt all along that the writers, individuals though they were, had not made their voices heard. "Now," he said, "is the time to raise our voices."

Someone suggested devoting next week's Talk of the Town to the crisis: "If they block printing that issue of Talk, we can just post it everywhere." People seemed to realize this would have no practical effect.

Mr. Shawn called, several times, on Lawrence Weshler, recently returned from Warsaw, to compare the situation to the crisis in Poland, and ask "what Solidarity would do." He called on John Brooks, the *New Yorker*'s writer on financial matters, "because he knows about business." Suddenly, Lillian Ross, in a throbbing voice, spoke up.

"Mr. Shawn," she said, and then repeated, "*Mr. Shawn*, maybe I'm stupid. I just want to say this, and then I'll shut up. I spoke to several people yesterday, and this morning, and they thought it was a good idea. The idea is to write a letter, from the whole staff, asking Bob Gottlieb to withdraw. And if he is the kind of man, who the people who *admire* him think he is, if he *understands* what the magazine *is*"—it now became apparent that she was addressing her remarks, not to the meeting at large, but in a challenging and even accusatory way, to a smaller group, including in particular Roger Angell—"he will understand the *letter* and withdraw."

Roger began his reply. "I assure you, Lillian, I feel as strongly about this as anybody here but, I'm telling you, I know Bob Gottlieb, and it isn't going to work." They had obviously already had this discussion and, just as obviously, disagreed. Chatter, incoherent muttering.

Ms. Ross's voice rose, several times, above the rest to say, "There are people here who *know* Bob Gottlieb," then subsided.

"I don't know him," Mr. Shawn said. "I've only met him twice. Once, when he was a child. And another time, just briefly. Of course, he's published several books by people from *The New Yorker.*"

"*After* they were edited here," Ms. Ross said. Mr. Shawn repeated, "After they were edited here." Ms. Ross's words were uttered derisively, with great scorn—and were not, of course, true. Shawn's tone was a mild echo.

"Well, *you people* know Bob Gottlieb," Ms. Ross said—again, apparently, to the small group of people, specifically including Roger. "Why don't you tell us, tell all of us here about him?" "I don't know him well," Mr. Angell said, a bit sullenly, "but I know people who do."

"Well," Ms. Ross said, "why don't *they* speak up then, and tell us what they think?"

Janet Malcolm said, "You're looking at me when you say that, Lillian. And I think the letter is a very good idea."

This was the turning point—all that demonizing history, Hitler, Lady Macbeth, the succession, the whole sequence of tensions within the magazine, brought to bear upon the moment. Janet Malcolm, one of the *New Yorker*'s most distinguished writers, a person of undeniable rectitude, decency, and manners, and married, of course, to Gardner Botsford (who, it now seemed more obvious than ever, would have been the ideal successor), happened to be a friend of Mr. Gottlieb's. She was also his neighbor. Their houses were yards apart in Turtle Bay. Mr. Botsford had already told friends he thought the firing was brutal and cruel, and that

Mr. Gottlieb was not the right man for the job. If Ms. Ross intended, as it appeared she had, a test of those she had long regarded as villains, Ms. Malcolm had risen to it. The question arose: Who would write the letter? Voices said that no one but Mr. Shawn could write what must be written. He recused himself.

"You write it, Roger," Ms. Ross said. Another old antagonist recruited.

Then the question: Who would edit it? "There are so many wonderful editors around here," Mr. Shawn said. "That shouldn't be any problem."

A person from makeup asked whether people who were not writers, artists, or editors, would be allowed to sign, and spoke of how honored they would feel to be allowed to sign it. A chorus, including Mr. Shawn, said, Of course they would be included—naming also other categories: checkers, messengers, and so on. A voice said, "Time is passing." Bill McKibben said, "It could be done and written in an hour." Another voice said, "That's Bill McKibben time."

Somebody mentioned, however, wanting to keep "the momentum" of this assembly, and there was in fact a conflict between a sense of urgency, the need to go at once and do something, and a sense of wanting to delay, to sustain this moment, of wanting to linger just to talk. The juggernaut for this preposterous idea, the letter, was now launched, it appeared, irremediably. The committee for drafting the letter was not so much appointed as acclaimed: Roger Angell, Janet Malcolm, Wen Weshler, John Brooks, Phillip Hamburger, and someone who did not usually hide but who seemed to be trying to fade back into the crowd as this went on, Calvin Trillin.

There were still little eddies of discussion and dissent. Anthony Hiss said, "Since this is serious, and people's livelihoods are at stake, we shouldn't decide hastily. We need time to reflect on what they are doing and what we ought to do." No one took this up, or appeared to hear or understand it. Jeremy Bernstein began his remarks: "There is no question Newhouse had the right to do this." That was ignored as well. Ms. Ross and several others had begun to preface their remarks with the words, "Time is passing," and "Since it is unanimous," and "Since we all agree."

A number of people spoke of getting the list of names out as fast as possible. Mr. Shawn said, several times, "The magazine is in jeopardy." The word "jeopardy" was taken up. Ms. Ross said, "We are fighting for our lives." She suggested "a voice vote of everybody here." Some people said they had proxies, for anything they might want to do, from writers who were abroad or absent for any other reason.

What was rolling now through the group was the notion that people should sign quickly, get those signatures, those names. I spoke up, at one point, saying that although I agreed it was important to use the momentum of this meeting for something, and to salvage the magazine, the letter under discussion seemed to me the wrong letter, with the wrong content, to the wrong person. I said again, in effect, what I had said to Ms. Ross, that if there were two distinct questions, the succession, and keeping Mr. Shawn as editor, there was no way to prevail on the first. On the second, the letter, if any, could be addressed to Mr. Newhouse, and the issue, which could be drawn, if necessary, as a resigning issue, confined to keeping Mr. Shawn.

"Since we're all agreed," Ms. Ross began.

"Maybe we should just walk out," one of the brave people from makeup said, "and found another magazine."

Ms. Ross smiled. "That comes later," she said.

She prefaced her next speech with the words "Since it's unanimous"—which, of course, it wasn't, although at moments, through the shutting down or ignoring of every dissenting or even doubtful voice, it did appear to be. The small space with agitated people in it was getting uncomfortably hot. Voices kept saying, "Time is passing." Also, that it was important to keep this discussion secret, above all from the press. Mr. Shawn said, "Nothing can be kept secret." No one should talk to the press, however, or, in phone calls, to anyone outside, "unless it's your wife," somebody added, "and you're calling to say you're late. But don't say why."

The group began to consider how and where the signing would take place. Mr. Shawn said this raised a question of confidentiality. Someone suggested there be a Yes list and a No list. "If one name appears on the No list, then the letter goes out without names, just the count of Yes and No." Ved Mehta said that the names were vital, what mattered was not quantity but the quality of the signers. That was shrugged off. Suddenly there was a wave of drama as people began to speak of "jobs at risk."

Mr. Angell spoke up. "People have been saying the main thing is to get those signatures fast," he said sensibly, "before the letter is even written. In that case, I'm not going to write it. People will be risking their jobs without having read what they signed." It was agreed that, after the committee finished drafting the letter, there would be another meeting, at five o'clock, for a reading of the draft.

For some time, it had been clear that, in this gathering, Ms. Ross was in command. The question again arose: who would edit the draft? Ms. Ross said, "It has to be Gardner Botsford." In other words, she had now brought in and implicated all her enemies in this disaster. Then people who chose to sign would sign, and the letter would go off.

It appeared that the course was set. It seemed that, with this one stroke, this preposterous letter—this single act of folly and discourtesy—the staff and its editor were about to foreclose any possibility of effective action. Resignations would no longer matter. In their doomed and moronic way, the meetings would make it impossible to take either Mr. Shawn or the *New Yorker*'s staff seriously again. With one stroke they had almost masterfully put themselves in the wrong, also hastened and made inevitable—even in some degree justified and made right—what it might still have saved the magazine to prevent: the dismissal and departure of Mr. Shawn. He was clearly getting old. He was still unsurpassed at meeting one person at a time. At meetings of this sort he was obviously no good at all.

On the way upstairs, I ran into Bud Trillin. "This is a disaster," I said.

"I know," he said. "I'll try to keep them from doing anything too wild."

"Just suppose Bob Gottlieb did withdraw," I said. "They're still not going to choose anyone from inside the magazine. It could be worse."

"I know," he said. "They could bring in some asshole from Condé Nast."

On the nineteenth floor, I met Jervis Anderson, a fine reporter, who had written a recent profile of A. Philip Randolph. Mr. Anderson said that, as the magazine's first and only black reporter since Charlayne Hunter, he could not sign a letter that appeared to consist of ganging up. He was worried about what his colleagues at the magazine would think about his not signing, but he could not sign. I asked what he thought of perhaps giving Mr. Shawn, instead, a letter with all the signatures in his pocket, which he could use in his negotiations, to stay as long as he liked. Mr. Anderson said he could sign that. He suggested we go in and talk about that with the committee, but we did not.

I found a message from Ms. Ross. I went to her office. She seemed conciliatory. I said, "See, I did speak up." She said, "We're neither of us good at public speaking."

I had a thought. I said, "Another way to go might be to

ask Bob Gottlieb to ask Mr. Shawn to stay on." I meant that Gottlieb would be designated successor, or the issue of succession could be postponed until Mr. Shawn retired. Ms. Ross misunderstood.

"That's a wonderful idea," she said. "A face-saving way. For Gottlieb to withdraw. A really face-saving way." She obviously meant, for Mr. Shawn to prevail and choose his successor, after all. She resumed the accusatory mode. "Why didn't you say that at the meeting?"

I said, "Well, I didn't think of it till now."

"Then go and tell them," she said. "Tell the committee now."

"I don't think I can do that," I said. "I didn't mean Bob should withdraw. I meant he could ask Shawn to stay on as editor. Bob could come in as his deputy and successor. I don't even know whether Bob would accept. Whatever Bob does, though, Shawn would have to give up on the succession, including Chip." She waved this off with both hands.

"Don't *worry*," she said. "It's just a face-saving maneuver. Gottlieb withdraws and asks Shawn to stay." She smiled. "And then we'll see."

I said I had to catch a train to Connecticut. "Come to the meeting at five o'clock," she said. I said I would.

In the hallway, on the way back to my office from another talk with Lee Lorenz, I passed Ms. Ross's office. With his back to me, his hand on the door, which was partly open, Mr. Shawn was leaning in. "I didn't catch what she said," he was saying, quite clearly, as I passed behind him. "Just something *political,*" Ms. Ross said, in a tone of absolute derision, "about Chip *McGrath.*" It was the only time in my life I have overheard something I was apparently not meant to hear.

I ran into Bob Shaplen, who agreed the letter was wrong —wrong content, wrong addressee, ganging up, and so on. We went together to see Bill Knapp, who listened, then said he and some others felt they had to sign, as veterans, to protect the jobs of the younger ones. He had already signed. I went into Pat Crow's office. He was at work on his vise for tying trout-fishing flies. He asked me for a Valium, mentioned the madness of things, and reminded me that we had both believed for years that the successor would be someone from outside. Pat and I went downstairs together. There were several small groups already gathered. One of the fluorescent lights had begun to flicker. I drifted toward the group nearest the exit, because I hoped to catch a train. I had already called my mother to postpone dinner, but I hoped to reach her house by eight.

Someone said copies of the letter, now called by some the "petition," were being made for everyone. I spoke with Andy Logan, who agreed the whole thing was madness, but who said that she and several older writers had discussed it, that they had lived their lives, brought up their children, sent them through college, and now felt, like Bill Knapp, that they should sign to protect the younger people. She looked around the group that was gathering—considerably fewer, it seemed to me, than at the earlier meeting. "There are some awfully nice people here," she said. Alison Rose (a fine writer, who was, at the time, the eighteenth-floor receptionist) said she preferred not to sign, and asked, only half-joking, whether I thought she would "incur the fear and loathing of my nearest and dearest" by not signing. I said I thought it was all right to sign or not to sign.

A little after five, the meeting began. Mr. Shawn, again on the third step, said he had "heard from people all over," spoken to "someone in Paris"—Mavis Gallant, perhaps, or Mary McCarthy. That person (it seemed there was no reason, really, not to say who it was) said she "would sign anything," and encouraged him to "call at any time of the day or night." He said that "someone very wise, who has been on the staff for many years," had come to see him at his office, and said that there was "a risk, in fact, maybe a certainty," that if Mr. Gottlieb did withdraw, Mr. Newhouse would appoint "somebody else, somebody worse," from outside, "but we must ignore that and do what we believe."

While the assembly was taking that in—while I was thinking what a very Shawn-like utterance it was—Mr. Shawn went on. He had also talked, he said, with "two people wise and experienced in diplomacy," who had told him that the decision was "irreversible." But, "We must ignore that too. We must not think of that, but do what we believe." I thought, Anyone who saw Mr. Shawn only in a group would not have reason to think highly of him. This was the language of high moral principle in the service of what? A kind of foolish and stubborn petulance. The owner of an enterprise, after all, was bringing in a highly regarded editor. The chief executive was insisting now on his own choice, an underling for whom he had never shown enthusiasm. In the name of this, the energies of a tribe of lemmings were being summoned to express, in writing, their position, whatever it was.

Sheila McGrath, a rather bossy office manager, said she had eighty-seven signatures in support and willing to be named, and one unwilling to be named. In that case, Mr. McKibben said, simply drop the unnamed one. All seemed to agree. Mr. Angell said that even members of the committee had not yet had a chance to sign. Others spoke again of proxies. Mr. Shawn said, "Be sure and get in touch with everyone. Call everyone who wants to sign it." Mr. Angell said the hall downstairs was "swarming with press." Several people urged everyone to say nothing to the press.

The question arose, whether or not to send the letter to the press before sending it to Mr. Gottlieb. "How did Newhouse do it?" a voice asked. Before telling Mr. Shawn, someone replied, Newhouse had sent his announcement to the press. "Then we should do it the same way."

"No, no," Mr. Mehta said. "Then you're being like Newhouse."

"Maybe send it confidentially and privately," said yet another voice.

"Nothing remains confidential or private," Mr. Shawn said.

Someone said, "The *Times* will get it anyway. Better send

it to them." Another voice: "Is there some way to get it to Gottlieb by this evening, and give it to the *Times* in the morning?" Somebody else: "But then he will have time to answer it." Still another: "Then both letters will appear in the *Times* at once."

Finally, it was decided that people would lobby for signatures, in the hour and a half after the meeting. A messenger would then take it to Mr. Gottlieb—and tomorrow to the *Times.*

Mr. Angell said that the letter had been, in every sense, a committee effort, that every member had made a contribution. Then he read the letter aloud. It was long. There was applause. I realized there was no way I could conceivably sign it.

When he finished, Ms. Ross, in her throbbing voice, said, "That *letter* could not have been *written* under Bob *Gottlieb.*" For some reason, this sentence, too—meaningless, perhaps, but undeniable—provoked appreciative laughter and applause.

There arose the question: In what order should the names be listed? "Alphabetically," a voice proposed. Ms. Ross nodded, vigorously. "Then the first name will be Roger *Angell,*" she said.

Mr. Shawn was now exhorting people to "call everybody." I started to leave.

On the way out, I picked up my messages at the reception desk. I went into my office to read them, letting the door close and, as it turned out, lock behind me. A knock at the door. "It's Brendan. Will you let me in?" I had wondered all day where Mr. Gill was. I opened the door. "I hear you spoke sanely this morning," he said.

"I'm afraid I can't sign it," I said.

"Of course, you can't," Brendan said. "Neither can I." We left the building together. There was no press in the hall that I could see. I called my mother from Grand Central and said that I was on my way.

From my mother's house, I called the Shawns' apartment. I reached Mrs. Shawn. She said she had a roast in the oven. We spoke at some length. I told her how moving I thought it had been, people filing down the stairs, trying to formulate a way to support Mr. Shawn. I could not think of much else to say. I found a message, on my answering machine, from Bob Gottlieb. I called him. "Do you want me to tell you about the meetings?" I asked.

"I am offended," he said. "Si is meeting with Shawn right now. It's got to be stopped, and stopped right now." I said that it was not so bad, that it could have been worse. It would be all right. There was only the letter, nothing compared to a strike, or whatever else there might have been. I said I had spoken at the meeting.

"Did you praise me to the skies?" he asked. I said I hadn't.

"I've been hearing all day," he said, "from people all over the world. I can't tell you, the warmth, the enthusiasm, the support. Not one person from *The New Yorker* has called me."

I said, "No one?" He said, "Not one." I said, "Well, I thought of calling you between the meetings, but it didn't seem—" He said, "I don't mean you." He spoke of the ingratitude of Jonathan Schell, for whom he said he had done a recent favor.

"I already know," he said, "that Roger Angell is behind it. Tell me one thing: Was Harold Brodkey there? Steve Florio says Shawn called me 'an evil presence' and said 'Watch out. He'll get you, too.' Tell me this, did Shawn mention, did he say one word about his compensation? You know, he lied about when he said he was going to retire."

"You know," I said, trying to think of something affirmative to say, "You ought to speak to Lee Lorenz. He is wonderful at what he does."

"Does he speak highly of me?" Mr. Gottlieb said.

Having, I thought, got the hang of this, I said, "Yes, he does. Very highly."

"I understand Chip speaks well of me," he said.

When I was back in my house in Newtown, Adam Gopnik called. He said that, apart from Martha Kaplan, Mr. Gottlieb's top assistant at Knopf, the only person Mr. Gottlieb would be taking from Knopf to *The New Yorker* was Mr. Gopnik. "You know, Bob did such a charming thing today at the office," he said. "Usually, when he passes my door, he points at me and says, 'You!' Today, when he passed, he said 'Toi!' I said, 'Moi?' And he said, 'Yes, toi! Or, as they would say at *The New Yorker*, Vous!' " He paused. "I'm told," he went on, "that Mr. Shawn said, 'The only good thing about all this is that Gottlieb is bringing Adam

Gopnik to *The New Yorker.*" He paused again. I thought, Perhaps he realizes that this is going a bit far. I waited.

"It's always been my dream to go to *The New Yorker,*" he said. "You don't think, do you, that the staff will think I'm Bob's catamite?"

Mr. Gottlieb's quote, in *The New York Times* of that day, included these words:

> I don't have lunches, dinners, go to plays or movies. I don't meditate, escalate, deviate or have affairs. So I have plenty of time.

The *Times* said he had used these words "in an interview several years ago," and chose to reaffirm them. The implication was that Mr. Gottlieb thought highly of this speech. It was just a quote, but it did not seem to bode so well.

Mr. Shawn's secretary, Laurie Witkin, called. The effect of the meetings on the eighteenth floor had been for Mr. Newhouse to accelerate Mr. Shawn's departure—reducing his remaining weeks at the magazine from six to two. I had wanted to see Mr. Shawn. I wasn't at all sure that he would want to see me. It turned out that he did. The first time he called me into his office was two days after the meetings. We did not talk long. He asked me about the Greg Rushford lawsuit. The suit had not yet been dismissed. The judge had already ruled that Mr. Shawn and I were out of the case, except as witnesses. I had gone to Virginia for my deposition.

"I can't go to Virginia," Mr. Shawn said. I said he didn't have to, that there was some doubt whether his deposition was required. The Newhouses had just won a case in which the government had sued them for eight hundred thousand dollars in estate taxes, by far the largest suit of its kind. I said I thought Leonard Garment, whom I had known for years and whom Condé Nast had assigned to us in the Rushford case, must have been the Newhouses' lawyer against the IRS. He said, Yes, when he realized that they had hired Garment for him, he was appalled. "I don't want to have a Watergate lawyer," he said. Then he asked me what I had really said at the meeting. "I didn't hear you," he said. "Nobody heard you. What did you say?"

I told him about my conversation with Jervis Anderson. I said I thought he could still go to Mr. Newhouse with everybody's signature in his pocket and, if he would just waive the matter of succession, salvage his editorship and the magazine. He sighed.

"I haven't given up," he said, "with Mr. Gottlieb or Mr. Newhouse." He clearly thought he might still prevail. And yet, as I was leaving, he asked me whether I was working on anything. I said I had tried a piece on modernism and feeling. "Get it in soon," he said.

Meanwhile, there was talk at the office of farewell letters, a farewell party. Jane Kramer was going to organize a jazz cantata. She called Whitney Balliett, the jazz critic, to consult him about it. Mr. Balliett suggested that she call Lillian Ross.

"What do you mean, party?" Ms. Ross said. "He's not

leaving." Ms. Ross told Andy Logan that she believed the whole notion of a party was an element of a Newhouse conspiracy to make Mr. Shawn's departure from the magazine appear a fait accompli.

The next time I went to see Mr. Shawn was two days before he left. I had brought with me a draft for Notes & Comment. I had not written one in years. This one, a piece about Mr. Shawn, had occurred to me when Janet Malcolm and I talked about writing him farewell letters. Ms. Malcolm spoke of how difficult these letters would be. "Shawn *knows* about writing," she said. That afternoon, Ms. Witkin talked about how strange it seemed that other publications were doing gossipy pieces instead of tributes. I said I had been called by *The Boston Globe* and *The Washington Monthly.* I hadn't returned their calls. "Maybe you should," Ms. Witkin said. Then she laughed. "As long as you don't say anything about how lovely Bob Gottlieb is." Anyway, she said, Mr. Shawn wanted to see me. I asked whether I might see him tomorrow. She said she was sure that would be all right.

"He even wanted to see you last week, but you had already gone." As we were talking, she excused herself, for a call on the other line. She said, "That's him. He definitely wants to see you." I asked her when Talk of the Town would be closing. She said Friday—but it could be held open until Monday morning. I told her about my draft for Notes & Comment. "Don't mention it to anyone," I said. "I'm only going to mention it to two people, you and him."

"I know about not telling people things," she said.

The next day, Thursday, February 12, 1987, I came in by train. Bill Knapp was in the same car. I had known vaguely that he was an editor, but I did not know whose work he edited, or what else he did. He said he used to edit Elizabeth Drew. I said I knew her fairly well. He said nothing. I said, "In real life, she seems a nice person." "In real life," he said, bitterly. "You know, she once dictated five columns to me, over the phone. Five solid columns." He said he now had a device on his phone that would make sure nothing like that ever happened to him again. I asked whether there had not been, even then, some technology that would have made it possible for Ms. Drew to do something other than dictate, at such length, to him. "Yes, there was," he said. "She could have brought it in herself." I laughed. I realized I was not meant to laugh.

When I reached the office, I called Ms. Witkin. I asked whether I should come in before or after lunch. She said after, "Before is when he sees Gottlieb, so you don't want that." I had lunch, at the Harvard Club, with Tony Hiss. "Did you ever wish, or do you sometimes wish, that your first job had been at some other magazine?" I asked. "Often," he said. We talked about what it might have meant to grow up at some other place. Then we spoke of Dorothy Dean, the first black member of the *New Yorker* staff, years before other magazines and newspapers had begun to hire black people in their editorial departments. Ms. Dean had also been the magazine's first female checker. Before that, she had been a classmate of John Updike's at Harvard, and a character in Cambridge for many years. Ms. Dean had the proverbial heart of gold—hidden under so many layers of caustic speech that it was amazing the magazine hired her at all. Her checking style was extraordinary. "That Ms. *Kramer claims,*" she would say, in sarcastic and accusatory tones, to the subject of a piece, "that you *said*"—and then make the quotation sound so idiotic that the subject felt inclined to deny he had ever said it. Most of the checkers, in those years, were gay. Ms. Dean would arrive, late, at her desk, in the large room the checkers occupied. She would begin with telephone calls to her friends. "I can't talk now," she would say, glaring at the checker nearest to her. "*It* is listening to me." After some years, she was fired—the first and only person, in Mr. Shawn's time, to be fired by the magazine.

When I arrived at Mr. Shawn's office, I was early. Ms. Witkin had her coat on. She said Mr. Shawn had gone to lunch. Did I want to wait in the chair beside her desk, as I had so often done when I was early. I said that would be nice. "Read the paper or something," she said. Then she left. I went to the ladies room. There were sheets on the bed there, striped brown, mauve, white, a bit disordered and unmade. I remembered when Edward Opie, the cartoonist, had moved his mother in there—also the more famous episode, when Maeve Brennan, a former wife of St. Clair McKelway's, and one of the most talented and prolific short story writers in the history of *The New Yorker,* had moved in. Mr. McKelway, a great friend, had also had famous periods of madness, which he used in his writing to wonderful effect. Editors often treat writers as though they are crazy, or children, or both. It occurred to me that the writers had been no crazier than the people in ostensibly more stable lines of work. One morning, Tom Gorman, the office manager in my early years, did not come to the office. It turned out that he had peed, the night before, all over the office of Rachel MacKenzie, a fiction editor. A rather schmoo-shaped messenger had drifted gradually, over a period of years, away from the magazine. A few months later, he was arrested for having dismembered a neighbor.

When I returned to Mr. Shawn's office, Ms. Witkin was on the phone. I left my coat on the usual chair, knocked, and went in. Mr. Shawn stood, as I came in—as, come to think of it, he always had. Apart from a fan on a table, the office was nearly empty. I shut the door behind me. I sat on the sofa. He sat on a hard wooden chair between the sofa and his desk. "First of all," I rather muttered, "it goes without saying, I love you and I hope to keep seeing you for the rest of our lives." He had interrupted, saying "I love you" quite firmly. When I said the words about seeing each other, he said, again firmly, "We will keep seeing each other." Then we were both in tears.

"What I realized long ago but then forgot," I said, "is that the magazine needs a genius. Now we haven't got one. They are going to discover within a few days that they can't run it without you."

"I don't suppose they're going to change their minds in

two days," he said. He seemed still to entertain the slightest, slimmest possibility that they might.

"I thought we could gain time," I said. "I thought you could stay. Apart from the moral and creative energy of the place, they're going to find they don't even know how it works."

"Not even technically," he said. "The process. The mechanics." He sat, with an arm on each arm of his chair, his head somewhat down.

"It's madness," he said.

"It was awfully violent."

"He hasn't asked anybody anything. He spent no more than five minutes a day with me. He's so restless. He can't stop going around, seeing people, never asking anybody anything, talking about himself. He has said—well, I can't properly tell you what he said. People are trying to be nice to him. I can't say it's encouraging. I can't say I'm optimistic."

I said I had asked Laurie Witkin whether it was too late for Notes & Comment, and that she had said no. It had been so long since I had written Notes & Comment, but yesterday, for the first time, I had an idea for one. I wondered whether it was too late, to write one about him.

"No," he said, "I don't see how I could edit it myself."

I said I wondered whether there wasn't some way to get around that. Maybe Gardner or somebody else could edit this one.

He said, "It's the anniversary issue."

I said I knew that.

He said, "Anyway, it's too late, on account of early closing."

"Well," I said, "I even thought of next week."

He said Mr. Gottlieb had already commissioned (assigned would have been his usual word; this time he said commissioned) a writer to do it. "But I told him the magazine traditionally doesn't write about people who don't want to be written about. I'm going to exercise the privilege and ask that the piece not be done."

I said I understood. There was intermittent stammering and hesitation, as there always had been in his presence—a shyness since I first came, which he of course had in some ways, as well. Although Lord knew, there had been other sides and interludes, perhaps in recent years sometimes predominating.

"Anyway," he said, "it would be an obituary, and it's not time for an obituary."

I said, "If I did it, it wouldn't be an obituary."

He said, "No, if you did it it wouldn't."

I said, "More of a statement."

He said, "I know what you would do. But also, I don't approve of what has happened, and permitting such a piece to appear in the magazine would imply . . ."

I said I could see that. "I wondered again and again," I said, "whether there was something we could have done that would have avoided this. Something that would have had a different outcome. I can't think of anything."

We talked about this for a while. I said, "Whether or not

there were mistakes, no matter what anyone did or could have done, it was probably inevitable from the moment they bought their first shares in the magazine."

"It was inevitable, from the first buying of the stock." He raised his head. "You know he did agree to Mr. McGrath."

We spoke almost in unison: "He never meant it"; "He didn't really mean it."

"After all," I said, "when he bought those first shares, he said it was only an investment. He said he had no intention of buying the magazine."

Mr. Shawn said, "And he didn't mean that either."

I had a thought. "Maybe," I said, "they were always planning to do it. Maybe they were going to do it right away, and were put off for two years." Meaning, they had intended to replace him at once but hadn't reckoned with how much they were going to respect him. He seemed to consider and even like this idea. "So maybe," I said, "these last two years have been a kind of miracle."

For a moment, he seemed bewildered, thinking I meant the new ownership itself.

I said, "I mean your having stayed," and he got it.

"In all my dread of whom they might put in," I said, "I forgot one. I forgot Clay Felker." Mr. Felker had once asked Kay Graham to buy the magazine for him. She wisely did not.

Mr. Shawn nodded.

"Of course, it might still happen," I said. "Or something like it."

"That is something that even Mr. Gottlieb would not know," he said.

"Everyone's going to continue to depend on you," I said. "It will be a burden; I don't know how it's going to work."

In this odd conversation, we were sometimes crying, sometimes not. At one point, he held out his hand, palm up, and I grasped it. I remembered that he had done the same, two years before—that he had extended his open hand for clasping, after the news that Si Newhouse had bought, or was going, finally and irrevocably, to buy the magazine. I thought, How fragile, after all, were the understandings of the man and his enterprise. I wished, not for the first and certainly not for the last time, that instead of saying, "He was one of the greatest editors in the history of American letters. If there had to be a successor, it should be Bob," I had said, in place of the second sentence, "And there can be no successor at all."

Whatever else we said, the conversation had curious asides. "Where will you be tomorrow?" he said, for instance. "Because I have a question which I want to ask our lawyer whether it would be proper to ask you." I never found out what that question was. Though the visit had been in no sense rushed, when I got up to leave, we embraced, for a long time, considering shyness, our whole history—even considering in retrospect, my handbag, which was somewhat in the way. We were both again in tears. Later, I remembered a story of a young woman, an employee in Edith Oliver's office, who had left, many years before, for another job. She felt she needed to say goodbye to Mr. Shawn. In his office, she had been overcome by such a long, intense, and utterly unaccountable fit of sobbing—she hardly knew Mr. Shawn, and had voluntarily taken the job elsewhere—that Mr. Shawn, in desperation, had called in Gardner Botsford. Mr. Botsford had led her, still sobbing, from the office, and taken her home in a cab. As I was walking across the carpet toward the door, Mr. Shawn said, "I'm not saying goodbye—to anyone. We'll see each other."

I opened the door. He stood, as he always did when someone left his office. From behind his desk, he said again, in a tone of surprising firmness and, considering the distance, gentleness, "I love you." I said again that I loved him. We shared a sense, I think, that since the day I first walked in and through the years, we were by temperament, style, understanding—through Hannah, Wally, Lillian, Mrs. Shawn, those birthday parties—family. I said, "See you soon."

On my way out, Laurie Witkin asked about the Notes & Comment. I shook my head, muttered, left. Otherwise, I didn't, obviously, stop to talk to anyone. The opening of my draft for Notes & Comment read, "It is not often that a genius in the arts is widely loved in his own time."

Chapter Seven

From the moment Robert Gottlieb arrived at *The New Yorker*, he threw into the sharpest possible relief three of Mr. Shawn's strongest qualities as an editor: his self-effacing style, his generous capacity for enthusiasm, and above all, his curiosity. It turns out curiosity—intense, varied, inexhaustible, almost without limit—is an indispensable quality in an editor of a publication. Book publishing may be different, more passive and selective. It may require other qualities. A book editor can, perhaps, wait to be amused. But the quality of being curious by nature—so that every subject, in every piece, in every issue, is an adventure—is a kind of courage of the spirit. In this respect, Mr. Shawn was very brave.

With regard to how the magazine was run, Mr. Gottlieb was almost comically incurious. People ranging from Mr. Shawn, through Lee Lorenz, even Chip McGrath, to every level of the magazine, complained that he never asked them anything, that he talked only about himself. This was not entirely true. He did talk about himself, but he also talked to other people, about themselves—almost always in a knowing, hardly ever in an inquiring, way. After every meeting with members of the *New Yorker* staff, he would say, "It went well. They think very highly of me"—when it hadn't gone well and they didn't. This might have seemed a touching kind of bravado, of whistling in the dark and trying to raise his own spirits. It seemed not. His voice was bored, his demeanor, languid. "He has absolutely no understanding of the magazine. He isn't interested. He doesn't listen," people said about him. "He keeps saying, 'What you see is what you get.' " Mr. Gottlieb, meanwhile, said, "The magazine doesn't require a full correction. Just a twenty-percent correction"; and, "I'm a quick study. I have a good sense of humor. I have a good eye. I just don't have a good visual memory"; and, "It's easy. The editors here don't really work. What is hard is Knopf. There's so much to do there"; and, "I knew on the third day I could do it. I'm happy. People love me. I've already weaned them from Mr. Shawn"; and, "What they don't realize over here is that Martha and Adam and I could do it by ourselves."

On a Wednesday in February, less than two weeks after Mr. Gottlieb's arrival at the magazine, I again had lunch with Lee Lorenz. Mr. Lorenz was worried. Mr. Gottlieb had already pulled several cartoons that would have been in forthcoming issues. He had given no indication of what he liked, or what he would do to replace them, except to say that he wanted "more Steinberg." The magazine had been trying for years to get more Steinberg. Mr. Lorenz then tried showing Mr. Gottlieb the complete range of work by every artist, trying to find out which side of any given artist he might like better than the cartoons he was rejecting. In every case, Mr. Gottlieb said he simply did not like the artist's work. Mr. Lorenz decided it was not fair to proceed in this way. He had been presenting the artists in alphabetical order. Mr. Gottlieb had been eliminating them alphabetically. As the art editor, Mr. Lorenz felt he had a responsibility to these artists. While he was trying to think what to do, Mr. Gottlieb suggested going back into the bank and killing drawings and cartoons. Mr. Lorenz pointed out that they were already paid for. He and Shawn had usually gone back in that way once every year, at the end of the year. Killing them sooner, he said, would narrow Mr. Gottlieb's choices. When he wanted to replace a cartoon or a drawing at the last minute, it might be hard to find one of the right size, or compatible with the issue in other ways. There were perhaps a thousand drawings in the backlog. Mr. Gottlieb now suggested that they kill between thirty and sixty a day.

A week later, Mr. Gottlieb told Mr. Lorenz that he had heard from a reader, who had noticed that the cartoons were already "fresher, funnier." "But, Bob, you didn't choose those," Mr. Lorenz said. They had been scheduled long ago.

"Well, this will shock them," Mr. Gottlieb said, pointing to a drawing he was about to select for the magazine's cover. "Well, yes," Mr. Lorenz said. "Our readers will certainly be shocked. They'll say, 'That's a Bob Gottlieb cover, all right.' " The drawing depicted the trunk and the stump of a recently felled tree, next to the head and body of a recently decapitated bird. To his credit, Mr. Gottlieb did not run the cover. To his credit, also, Mr. Gottlieb sometimes gave intimations of the judgment and the more nuanced character he had shown before his appointment to the magazine. To Ms. Malcolm, he said that she ought to think of some of his utterances as irrepressible "exhaust," and to disregard them. The difficulty was that the utterances were so unfortunate and so frequent. A greater difficulty was that many people were not free to disregard them, for the most obvious reason: his powers as their boss and editor.

The source of power in any magazine, of course, originates in the talents of the people who create it. Without consolidation in the power of an editor, however, his intuition, tact, judgment, and capacity to inspire, those talents will not see the light of day. As an enterprise grows, accumulating resources and staff, it becomes harder, particularly for an editor whose gifts are not primarily administrative, to deal directly with his creative people. The issue of power at *The New Yorker*, even under Ross and Shawn, had always been vexed and uncomfortable. When a writer once mentioned to Jonathan Schell that courtiers at the magazine were maneuvering for power, he shuddered. "We don't mention that word around here," he said. The yeomen, under Gottlieb, worked in obscurity to preserve the magazine. The courtiers worked, for power, on the editor.

That section of the bureaucracy which had devoted years

to the succession, and to flattering Mr. Shawn, found Mr. Gottlieb an easy mark. He liked to say that Mr. Shawn had treated people shabbily, while he, Mr. Gottlieb, had at once recognized their talents—permitted them, for example, to help him with the technical aspects of putting out the magazine. Mr. Shawn, meanwhile, had installed himself, across the street, in the Algonquin. From there, he was secretly and patiently editing those sections of the magazine which the staff members whose competence Mr. Gottlieb esteemed so highly had no idea how to edit. They brought the unedited copy to Mr. Shawn—complaining about Mr. Gottlieb as they went. Then they brought the edited copy back to makeup, and to Mr. Gottlieb. Members of the staff who had not taken part in any schemes for the succession went on with their work, unrecognized.

William Hamilton, a friend and a wonderful cartoonist, described even Mr. Lorenz, in the years after Mr. Shawn, as a Quisling. He did not seem like a Quisling to me. "Just last week, I told my wife I was wondering whether I could keep my job," he said. "Last night I was wondering whether I even want to." In a note from that period, I found myself, too, comparing the position to a country under occupation.

> The occupiers seem quite giddy, imagining themselves liberators, thinking, and telling everyone how much they are esteemed and loved. The place meanwhile is full of collaborators and concierges. Perhaps, though by no means certainly, there are outlying cadres of Re-

> sistance fighters. More probably, not. Still, there's Shawn at the Algonquin, a most peculiarly placed de Gaulle.
>
> At the same time, the place has the air of a shabby boarding school—*sans* headmaster, *sans* faculty or curriculum. There is just the dormitory, run by prefects—complete with hazing, and a kind of undeclared, bullying homosexuality.

In the third week, I went to see Bob Gottlieb in his office. There was a wreath, containing, among other objects, tennis balls tinted an electric blue, from his friends the Sterns—writers with whom he had always shared certain camp enthusiasms: flea market knickknacks, plastic handbags, visits to Graceland. The door was open. His desk was against a wall to the right of the doorway. Just in front of the door, facing his desk, was an empty chair. As I walked in, I started to shut the door behind me.

"Don't," he said.

"Don't what?" I said.

"Don't close it. I hate closed doors."

"Bob," I said, "people can see into your office from all the way down the hallway. They can't see you or your desk. They just see who is in your office, sitting in this chair, in profile."

"I know," he said. "In my office at Knopf, they could see me and everything that was going on." I remembered that was true. He had not, I noticed, brought from his office at Knopf an immense white porcelain she-wolf with dugs.

"Joseph Heller said it, in *Catch-22.* The worst thing is closed doors."

I said that surely Joe Heller was speaking somewhat metaphorically—surely he hadn't meant all closed doors, always. I thought, Quite apart from what it means in literary or professional terms, this immediately turns the office into a performance, a spectacle, a source of gossip and a piece of theater. In politics, open town meetings and other public forums are important. It is also nice for employees to think the boss's door is open to them. Once they enter, however, the door must shut. Adult conversation, any real conversation, takes place behind closed doors.

I said I thought people might feel self-conscious, being seen, in profile, from the end of the corridor. Every visit would be subject to comment and speculation. I asked whether I might lean the door to. "All right," he said. He winced when I did it.

He stood, fiddling with a shade, then pointed to a bulletin board, with many numbers, labelled Back of the Book. "Shall I tell you what they are?" he asked. He moved around the office, adjusting objects. Finally, he sat down. I had brought one of my scripts, a list of things I meant to ask or say. I took it out of my pocket. He said, "You know what makes me want to kick ass?" The expression seemed uncharacteristic of him. I said, "No. What?" He had heard, he said, that some writers were not going to the annual office party. I said that did not seem to me unusual. The event was essentially an advertising party. Writers went, in their early years, to get something to eat. After that, they did not usually go except in special years. In 1966, for instance, there had been the *New Yorker*'s fortieth anniversary party. Even that was an odd occasion. No one was allowed to bring a guest, no significant others, not even wives. Mr. Shawn, however, had permitted, perhaps even invited, the photographer Jill Krementz to come, with the result that everyone, including Mr. Shawn, was photographed, many times—which made it hard to see why no one else was allowed in.

"This is a boycott," Mr. Gottlieb said. "They're children. It's the only thing so far that has made me want to kick ass."

Since he came to the magazine, Mr. Gottlieb seemed to have acquired a little reflex of quarrelsomeness. He had begun, often, instantly to contradict or to argue with what had just been said, even when he said it himself. He showed me a Notes & Comment he had written. "Someday I'll tell you about all that," he said. I said that perhaps he should keep a journal. "I could never criticize Shawn," he said. I said I thought there was no need to criticize Mr. Shawn. "I meant that as a criticism," he said.

He asked me what I thought of Elizabeth Drew's Letters from Washington.

"Well, I think in real life she is a nice person," I said.

"I don't think she's a nice person," he said. "She is well-connected. I called Meg Greenfield, and she said that much." I thought, He doesn't understand the influence and the ramifications of the Washington correspondent's job any better than his own. The editor of *The New Yorker* will inevitably be treated in certain ways by his staff, and the magazine's Washington correspondent will be well-connected. It is the nature of the institution.

Mr. Gottlieb said he needed pieces. "I was thinking," he said, "there is no way anyone can impede me, except by quitting or if they stop producing." I said I had always heard, or the legend had always been, that *The New Yorker* had such a backlog of first-rate pieces that it could run for ten years without buying one more. In fact, Walter Pincus, some years before, had proposed to Mr. Shawn the publication of a new magazine, which Mr. Pincus would edit, that would consist almost solely of work *The New Yorker* had bought but would never run. Mr. Shawn had said no, that he was planning to run it all. Mr. Gottlieb now said there was no such backlog. He offered me the Press column. I thanked him and said I couldn't do it. I looked at my script. I suggested that a good writer for the Press column would be Maureen Orth. "I know her," he said. "She's kind of a lightweight, don't you think?"

I said I thought that the staff and the magazine of late had undergone a decline in vitality. "That's already lifting," he said.

Off stride by now, I started to say something grandiose about "one of the most brilliant periods in the history of the magazine." With that reflex of dispute, he interrupted. "I don't know about brilliant. Fifty-two issues a year can't be brilliant. If it's ordinary or acceptable, that's good enough." We were silent for a minute. "I spent more time with Mr.

Shawn in the last week than anyone else ever has," he said. "I went to see all the editors, which is apparently a first." I thought, Surely even he does not believe either of these sentences. I let it pass. Mr. Gottlieb said he had offered Janet Malcolm the Television column. She had turned it down. Did I want it? I thanked him. I had had the column for two years. I didn't know or care much about television any longer. I suggested one of the *New Yorker*'s best writers, and its best-known television critic, Michael Arlen. Mr. Gottlieb said No, and gave various reasons. I said I would like to review a recent book, by Seymour Hersh, about Henry Kissinger. "You didn't like it," he said. I said that was true. He said, "It will be like your book, or your piece about Pauline Kael. I agreed with you. I hate journalists, but you would go for the jugular." I said that might be true. I would like to do a reporting piece, then, about Henry Kissinger—although there might be a problem, in that he had become a friend. Mr. Gottlieb said he hated Kissinger.

"He's vain. He may even be a war criminal. If there's one thing I can't bear," he said, "it's vanity." I put away my script.

Mr. Gottlieb said, "You know, you were a pet of Shawn's. For your sake, I don't want you to be perceived of as my pet."

As I thought that over, the door opened. Adam Gopnik came in. Not having seen me, of course, on account of the door leaning shut, he was stooped, literally rubbing his hands together, and blinking against the light from the windows behind Mr. Gottlieb's desk. He had a few days' growth of beard. As his vision adjusted, he was astounded and clearly appalled that Mr. Gottlieb already had a visitor. If there had been music, it might have been a moment in a horror film. He walked a few steps, leaned over my chair. I kissed him on the cheek. He looked only at Mr. Gottlieb. "I would like to do a Talk piece," he said, "about the Fashion Institute of Technology."

With stammers, little laughs, upward puffs of air, and this new rubbing of the hands, he described what he had in mind. Mr. Gottlieb heard him out.

"Do it," he said. "If it's good, we'll print it. If it's not good, we'll shoot it down."

Mr. Gopnik left, rather meaching, as he had been when he came in. He left the door open. A small silence. "Adam is adorable," Mr. Gottlieb said.

In the event, the birthday party did not become an issue. Mr. Gopnik did go. He had called me, he said, to ask my advice about going, and about some other developments in his career. He had written a piece, about Seurat, and submitted it to *The New York Review of Books.* Robert Hughes, the art critic of *Time,* had "implored" him to call Barbara Epstein, and ask her, on Mr. Hughes's behalf, to publish the piece soon—so that Mr. Hughes could "refer to it in his speeches." Did I think he should call Ms. Epstein, or might it be misunderstood? Mr. Hughes might be coming as art critic to *The New Yorker.* If he did, Mr. Gopnik said, he was going to recommend Mr. Gopnik as his successor at *Time.* So Mr. Gopnik felt he owed Mr. Hughes, at least, the call to Ms. Epstein. Which led him to another question. John

Russell, the art critic of *The New York Times,* was about to retire. He had offered to recommend Mr. Gopnik as his successor at the *Times.* If he were offered the art critic's job at *Time, The New York Times,* and also—as Mr. Varnedoe and other members of what Mr. Gopnik now called "my board of directors" believed was extremely likely—*The New Yorker,* which one should he choose? And should he, meanwhile, call to encourage Mr. Russell, or tell him about "my other options"? Was I going to the party? Did I think he should go?

I had begun, if not to dread, at least to hope to avoid these conversations. After our meeting in Mr. Gottlieb's office, Mr. Gopnik, I knew, had called Avedon, to ask, "How did Renata's meeting with Bob go?" Mr. Gottlieb had shown me a Notes & Comment he had written. He seemed touchingly, obviously proud of it. It occurred to me that one virtue Mr. Gottlieb did seem to have in abundance, and to have preserved in his transition to the magazine, was lack of hypocrisy. This was not quite the same as that positive, dangerous virtue, sincerity. It may even have grown out of a fault: an apparently absolute lack of self-doubt or self-criticism. But hypocrisy is a key strategy of the bureaucrat, and Mr. Gottlieb, for whatever reason, did not have it. With few exceptions, people associated with the magazine, or who wanted to be associated with the magazine, at this juncture, did have it. One exception was Martha Kaplan, the assistant whom Mr. Gottlieb had brought to the magazine. She was not insincere or hypocritical. She was nice. At the same time, she saw some things clearly. She said that she was uncomfortable with people who were immediately disloyal, that among members of the old staff she preferred people like Martin Baron, the head of the checking department, who was somewhat aloof. "It's all right to go to Shawn complaining about Bob," she said. "But not the other way around." Mr. Gottlieb, by contrast, was saying, "For your ears only: You would be surprised how many people, under their layer of love of Shawn, are in fact deeply angry with him, and I can see why." Another exception was Gardner Botsford, who actually wrote a letter to Mr. Gottlieb, proposing a "Zen exercise"—namely, to go through a period of time without saying "I." Mr. Botsford said his letter was "a hard one to receive." "If I had received a letter like that I couldn't continue to be the same person."

"But he came to you to edit his Talk piece," I said—meaning the Notes & Comment which Mr. Gottlieb had showed me at the office.

"He came to show it to us, just for our approval," Ms. Malcolm said. "He was surprised when Gardner vanished into the other room with it. When Gardner reappeared, with almost everything crossed out, Bob was appalled. He said he would have to exercise his writer's right to reject the editing. Then Chip edited it down further, and that is what ran." Ms. Malcolm had already written Mr. Gottlieb a note, saying they could no longer discuss the magazine. She wondered whether she should write him another letter, saying they could no longer be friends. I said my problem was that, "against my better judgment, I somehow always fawn."

"Maybe that's why he likes us. He wanted our approval and we never gave it," Ms. Malcolm said. We considered, almost seriously, whether Ms. Malcolm should write him a fawning letter, in which case he would drop or reject her ("and what a relief that would be"), and I should write him an attacking letter, in which case he would respond favorably. I did not really fawn. It took me a little longer than Mr. Botsford or Ms. Malcolm, not exactly to be frank, but in most ways to be gone.

I had learned over the course of conversations with Mr. Gopnik that his questions were not questions, or even quite soundings. Their purpose was to maneuver you into advising him to do what he would, in any case, walk over corpses to do. Even I could not bring myself, however, to say, Yes, do call Barbara Epstein, as a favor to Bob Hughes, so that she will publish your piece so he can refer to it in his speeches. Yes, do, or no, do not call John Russell about your "other options." This may, in fact, have been a pivotal moment in my conversations with Mr. Gopnik, and in my relationship with what the magazine had now become. Mr. Gopnik had already told me that he was saving the tapes of messages on his answering machine, and filing them each night. I was also familiar with his use of the word "implored." The authors Wilfred Sheed and Conrad Richler had implored Mr. Gopnik to leave *GQ* for Knopf. Mr. McGrath and Ms. Epstein had implored him to send them pieces. Joseph Mitchell and Saul Steinberg had implored him to edit their work. Ought I now to seem to implore Mr. Gopnik to call, if not Ms. Epstein, then at least Mr. Russell, to describe what he called his options? To go to the office party? The question, I realized, was meaningless. I would be described as having implored him to do whatever he did.

"I think I must go to the party," Mr. Gopnik said. "I think it would be mean-spirited not to." He said he had written his first Notes & Comment. It was a breakthrough, he said, the best thing he had ever done. "It has become the talk of the magazine." Not a Jonathan Schell piece, then, I said. "Well, oddly enough, it is a sort of allegory of Jonathan Schell, a fourth-century fable about the Holocaust, Star Wars, and SDI. I think it's important to keep the continuity." I thought, Good grief.

Mr. Gopnik called Avedon. "It seems I'm ruffling feathers," he said. "Chip came by and said Bob has not been fair to me, setting my Notes & Comment so soon. He should have waited at least a month, for me to get the tone right." Mr. Gopnik showed the piece to Avedon. Avedon said he thought the beginning was pretentious. "Bob refused to let me cut the beginning," Mr. Gopnik said. Avedon said he thought the ending was awful. "Bob wrote the ending," Mr. Gopnik said. Avedon asked what had happened to the

Fashion Institute of Technology piece. "Chip and Roger came to see me about it," Mr. Gopnik said. "They said it was too faggy."

The next morning, Mr. Gopnik called me, about the party. "It was good," he said. "Jonathan Newhouse was there, and people were ragging him. They were saying, 'Sit up straight, Jonathan. Speak when you're spoken to, Jonathan.' "

I said, "They were?"

He said, "Yes. It was good they felt free to do that. Jonathan spoke highly of Bob. He said he was in awe of him. They said, 'Jonathan, what would you do if he published the Oslo telephone directory?' I think he regretted his answer the minute it slipped out. It's obviously the influence of his family. He said, 'We would fire him.' "

I asked Mr. Gopnik whether he had taken part in this "ragging." "No," he said. "I was talking to Si." He went on to say that he had written yet another Notes & Comment, this one about boxing. "If I may say so," he said, "my piece points in a whole new direction. I have been thinking. There are a lot of good writers here. There is no reason why they can't do something like this every week." I wondered, not for the first time, Is this pathology, or the wave of the future?

I was about to end the conversation. Mr. Gopnik said, "Let's have dinner. You could stop by my office." A pause. "Or I could come to yours." At the time, I knew, Mr. Gopnik had the office of the jazz critic, Whitney Balliett, whom Mr. Gottlieb had just fired. Saul Steinberg asked him what floor his office was on. "The nineteenth," Mr. Gopnik replied. "Good," Mr. Steinberg said. "That is the chic floor." Several weeks later, when Lillian Ross left the magazine, Mr. Gopnik moved into her office. He stayed there. I said I couldn't have dinner because I was planning to stay for a while in Connecticut. "Can we talk now?" Mr. Gopnik said, "About the magazine? I'm eager to hear your impressions."

I said I thought it was amazing how rapidly things had changed, how much the situation and the magazine had changed already.

"Could you expand on that a little?" he said.

"Well, apart from a thousand things Bob couldn't know," I said, "and that he doesn't know who would tell him, the magazine itself is not the same. It's already a Condé Nast publication—but with typos, cartoons missing their captions, hideous ads. A friend of mine received an issue missing several pages. Then the prior pages were repeated. The price per issue has been raised. There's a new section, in *New Yorker* type, advertising real estate. And the pieces are not good. It's something that in all one's fears, hopes, and analyses, one could not have predicted, even a short time ago."

"Five years ago?" Mr. Gopnik asked.

"Two weeks ago," I said. "It's not even a first-rate Condé Nast publication. Whatever else it is, it is irremediably not the same." Mr. Gopnik sighed.

"Yes," he said, as though he were agreeing with every word and nuance of what I had just said. "It has become a better magazine. But not as nice a place to work in. And that's sad."

One afternoon, not long afterwards, I went to see Rupert Murdoch. I said that if he were to start a magazine, I thought I would be able to abscond overnight with all the valuable members of the staff of *The New Yorker*—writers, editors, cartoonists, workers of every other kind—and that, on the following morning, neither the people at Condé Nast nor Mr. Gottlieb, who seemed to value other people entirely, would realize that they, and effectively the magazine, had gone. We talked about what the new magazine might be, very like *The New Yorker*, in most respects, except that, politically, it would be a magazine a Republican could read, without being made to feel like an unenlightened and fundamentally second-rate citizen. Mr. Murdoch was not just courteous. He was ahead of me in the entire conversation. A pause came over only two questions: Who would edit the magazine, and what would it be called? I had somehow not thought of these. We never discussed the matter again.

With time, Mr. Gottlieb's style and manner at the magazine improved. His self-confidence, however, and lack of curiosity led to all sorts of difficulties with, to take but one example, Steven Florio. "If you do this," Mr. Gottlieb once said to Mr. Florio, "you will be a hero. And I want you to be a hero." The heroism Mr. Gottlieb was asking for consisted in ceding to the editorial department a fraction of certain columns which, Mr. Gottlieb believed, had always belonged to advertising. Mr. Florio reluctantly agreed. Mr. Gottlieb spent days, and stayed up overnight, "wrestling," as he said, to cut two columns out of advertising's space. Then he profusely praised the heroic Florio. The space in question, however, had always belonged to the editorial department of the magazine. Sections of it had in fact been turned over, on rare occasions, to the advertising department but only at the editor's absolute discretion.

In this period, the magazine began, for the first time in forty years, actually to lose money. Advertising fell twenty-five percent, the first precipitous phase in what became its long decline.

Adam Gopnik, meanwhile, was becoming the editorial counterpart of Steven Florio, or perhaps a New York incarnation of Widmerpool, the character in Anthony Powell's *Dance to the Music of Time,* who embodies certain lamentably ascendant qualities of his time. Within weeks, Mr. Gottlieb had appointed him culture editor. Mr. Gopnik wrote sections into other people's pieces. Writers objected. Mr. Gottlieb persuaded Mr. Gopnik to resume his own writing full-time. Stefan Kanfer, a friend and former colleague of Robert Hughes, called me. He had had lunch with Art Cooper, the editor of *GQ.* Mr. Cooper said Adam Gopnik had told him not only that Bob Hughes was recommending him as his successor at *Time,* but that Mr. Gottlieb as well was planning, when he left *The New Yorker,* to recommend

Mr. Gopnik to succeed him. Mr. Kanfer had also heard from Bob Hughes, who said he might indeed leave *Time* for *The New Yorker.*

"He's already recommended his successor," Mr. Kanfer said. "It certainly isn't Adam Gopnik."

A few days later, Brooke Hayward called. Ms. Hayward, her husband, Peter Duchin, and I had once organized a Bible study group. We were close friends. They were also close to Bob Hughes. He had decided not to come to *The New Yorker,* Ms. Hayward said. He didn't trust the Newhouses. Instead, his brother, whom she described as "a hotshot lawyer," was flying over from Australia to negotiate the best possible deal with *Time.* Then Avedon called.

"Adam feels really betrayed and hurt," he said. "Hughes is not coming to *The New Yorker.* Adam feels used."

"I don't understand," I said. "How does Adam come into it?"

"Adam feels he really went to bat for him," he said. "He feels betrayed."

"By Hughes?" I said. "Surely, Bob Hughes didn't need Adam to go to bat for him at *The New Yorker.*"

"Well, he feels used. Adam has this new thing. He's worried about the magazine, and how it would look if word now gets out that people are not coming to *The New Yorker.*"

"You don't think there's some self-interest here? Adam said they were friends. He said Hughes was going to recommend him as his successor at *Time.*"

"He said friendship doesn't come into it. He says what matters now is the welfare of the magazine."

I said, "I see."

What had begun was a pattern, on Mr. Gopnik's part, of letting it be known, shyly and modestly, or otherwise, that he was responsible, behind the scenes, for events in other people's professional lives. The *New Yorker*'s invitation to Hughes was just one example. In a way, I was another. Mr. Gopnik once asked Mr. Kanfer, "What did you think of Renata's book?" "I liked it," Mr. Kanfer said. "She's a close friend of mine." "I'm so relieved," Mr. Gopnik said. "I edited it." He subsequently led Avedon to believe that his "going to bat" for Avedon had persuaded Tina Brown to hire him as the magazine's photographer. Perhaps more typically, and more egregiously, in a review of a volume of John Richardson's work on Picasso, Mr. Gopnik claimed to have made, when he was a student, what he described modestly as a "small discovery"—a previously undiscovered symbol in Picasso's work. The discovery was in fact a small one, but Mr. Gopnik did not make it. Linda Gasman, a Ph.D. candidate at Columbia, made it, and gave extensive space to it, in a doctoral thesis, widely circulated at the Institute of Fine Arts, where Mr. Gopnik was a student. Most recently, David Remnick was appointed editor of *The New Yorker* after submitting to Si Newhouse a memo of several thousand words about what he would do to improve the magazine. Mr. Gopnik let it be known that he, with the help of a friend, Henry Finder, had written the memo, and that Mr. Remnick owed his appointment to them.

Within the first few months of Mr. Gottlieb's tenure, President Reagan nominated Robert Bork to replace Justice Powell on the Supreme Court. I had met Judge Bork when he was a professor at the Yale Law School. I had no courses with him. I had no reason to think less than highly of him. He was a friend of friends. Then I began to read his works. I became convinced that I was the only one who had ever read nearly all of them. They were beyond belief. They were not only unworthy of a candidate for the Supreme Court; they seemed to disqualify him as any sort of constitutional scholar, and to cast doubt on his qualifications to teach either at Yale or at the University of Chicago Law School, where he had also held a professorship. In a piece about the constitutionality of laws banning contraception of any kind, he had written, for example, that, just as there exists, in the matter of zoning, a right to frame statutes that ban factories from residential areas—on the grounds that their smoke pollutes a homeowner's air—there exists a right to frame statutes that ban contraception, on the grounds that the thought of neighbors using contraception may pollute that homeowner's mind. "The cases are identical," he wrote.

No one to whom I have quoted this has believed that Judge Bork actually wrote or published such a view. They usually think he was somehow unjustly denied his seat on the Court. But Bork so liked this argument, and this analogy, that he actually used them twice, in two different publications, the *Indiana Law Review*, and the *Colorado Law Review*. Right down to "The cases are identical." And other arguments, on other matters, equally bizarre. The notion that he was a strict constructionist, in constitutional matters, turned out to be untenable, to an almost laughable degree.

I told Mr. Gottlieb I thought *The New Yorker* should devote all of Talk of the Town to Notes & Comment, and all of Notes & Comment to the issue of Judge Bork. Mr. Gottlieb initially said "No. For two reasons: We would be wrong; and it can't be won." I wrote a piece, and managed to persuade him. Then trouble set in. I had become accustomed, under Mr. Shawn, to revising proofs until the final deadline. The checking department, however, had become accustomed, under Mr. Gottlieb, to regarding its function as largely editorial. While Mr. Gottlieb and a checker, then, indulged in discussions of whether the word "very," in context, was justified, and whether some adjective was "fair," time passed. As the deadline approached, the checker realized he had almost no time left for facts. "I can't find it," he would say, with verifiable dates and lines. The process had profoundly changed. The piece ran. I did not care for it. I wrote another, on the same subject, for Leon Wieseltier at *The New Republic*. That piece ran too. Mr. Gottlieb and I remained friends. For whatever reason, during his tenure, I did not write for *The New Yorker* again.

Chapter Eight

In the first months of Mr. Gottlieb's editorship, I had lunch with Mr. Shawn at the Algonquin. We talked a bit about the magazine. He said he could not look at it. I knew he was still editing whatever sections were brought to him. He said that was different. I asked whether he thought it would be crazy for me to try to write a book about *The New Yorker.* "I don't think that would be crazy at all," he said. "I'll help you with it." I knew him better than to count on that. I asked whether he would be writing something of his own. "I could never write about the magazine," he said. "The magazine speaks for itself, in every issue. For me to write about it would be redundant." I said I had never before understood people who said of a love affair, any emotional experience, when it was over, that they could not remember what the source of all that emotion was. I now felt that way about *The New Yorker.* I could not remember what I ever saw in it. "Because it's changed," he said. "It is hard to recognize." For the rest, we spoke of a German children's book, which my mother had just translated; of writing fiction; and of S. N. Behrman, whom he said he loved. Later that afternoon, I told Lee Lorenz about our lunch. He asked about Mr. Shawn. I said he seemed sad but resigned. "That's good," he said. "Jonathan had lunch with him last Thursday. He said the same. But when I had lunch with Shawn, he talked about getting people to march on Newhouse's office and asking him to reverse his decision." Mr. Shawn, apparently, had not quite given up.

Wallace Shawn had written a wonderful play, *Aunt Dan and Lemon,* which made extensive, largely negative references to Henry Kissinger. Wallace initiated an exchange of letters. They agreed that I might arrange a lunch. We met at the Four Seasons. It was a fine lunch, remarkable to me, by then, for its open-mindedness and humor. Humor had entirely vanished—it seems, in retrospect, permanently—from the magazine. I was working on a long piece about the Bilderberg Meetings, an international conference, hardly ever mentioned in the press, that had been held on at least one weekend every year since 1954. Henry Kissinger was on the steering committee. As all participants are supposed to do, he refused to talk about it. Vernon Jordan, too, was on the steering committee. I had known him as a Civil Rights leader, in the sixties. Now he was an attorney in Washington, for, among others, Dwayne Andreas. This was 1987, five years before Bill Clinton was elected president. I took Vernon Jordan to lunch.

"What do you want to write about the Bilderberg for?" Mr. Jordan said. "It's not important. It's boring. Why don't you write about something people are interested in? Just the other day, I sent my secretary out to get a piece about that couple, what is their name?"

"The Gutfreunds?" I asked.

"Right," he said. "Why don't you write a piece about something like that?" I said that perhaps I did not write the sort of pieces he sent his secretary out for. If Bilderberg was unimportant, why was he on its steering committee, and why did he travel to attend its meetings, year after year. "I'm into bullshit, alright?" he said, crossly. He paid the check for lunch. Of course, a piece of the sort Mr. Jordan was suggesting was out of the question for *The New Yorker* even in Bob Gottlieb's time.

Harriet Walden was, for many years, Mr. Shawn's secretary. Before that, she had been Harold Ross's secretary. Before *that,* her husband, William Walden, was Mr. Ross's secretary. When Mr. Walden went off to World War II, Mrs. Walden took his place. Under Bob Gottlieb, *The New Yorker* had donated its archive to the New York Public Library. I began to go with Mrs. Walden, sometimes daily, sometimes sporadically to look at it. The archive was a scandal. Several hundred linear feet of documents had been lost, in transit from the *New Yorker*'s offices on Forty-third Street to the library on Forty-second. The introduction, the chronology and guide to the documents, was, by turns, superficial, uninformed, inaccurate, and plain wrong. Documents which should have been in the archive, including pieces that actually ran in the magazine, were not in it. Documents which did not belong in the archive, letters from applicants rejected for jobs, rejected manuscripts, were there in profusion. A lot of material was misfiled. The archive was housed in a special, climate-controlled room. The library staff in charge of the archive, which was thought to be shorthanded, was actually too numerous, and mostly unobliging. Harold Ross's files were there. The index, according to its lists of boxes, was under the impression that Mr. Shawn's files were there as well. Mr. Shawn's files were not in those boxes, or anywhere. Mr. Shawn, with Laurie Witkin's help, had wisely removed them. It is not clear that they still exist. If they do exist Wallace and Allen Shawn will presumably one day have them. But it is almost the ultimate of the ironic echoes that the *New Yorker*'s archive would so mock the values of the magazine. Inaccuracy, indiscretion—all the violations of privacy implicit in making accessible, of all things, rejections, of pieces and of applicants. It is as if the archive itself were a joke. In view of the indiscretion, inaccuracies become almost a redeeming feature.

Under Bob Gottlieb, the magazine had begun seriously to slide. One problem, which I remembered from the early, dreadful days of *Vanity Fair*, was the problem of the claque. The claque seems to come not just with power but with celebrity or notoriety of any sort. People with a certain fortunate disposition tend to believe their claque and even quote it. Richard Locke, then Leo Lerman, and even Alex Liberman were always pulling out of their pockets letters of fulsome praise from writers, artists, critics (including, as it happened, Robert Hughes), without any apparent awareness that this was not what the same people were saying in the outside world. What they were hearing was just the voices of the claque. For people who are subject to self-doubt, or who do not hear the claque or heed it, or who even hear the other side's claque, the world is a less welcoming place. On the other hand, they may pay closer attention to the real quality of their work.

The sharpest decline in the magazine under Gottlieb occurred in non-fiction. The whole form of the Profile changed. Its conventions and understandings were eroded. Non-fiction pieces, as soon as they came in, were thought to be in need of cutting. This assumption, that every article as written is too long and requires cutting, is held by editors at many, perhaps most, magazines. It had generally been conceded that *New Yorker* pieces were too long. This was often true. But the explanations for an impatience with length—that readers were too busy, that there was too much to read, that a post-McLuhan, MTV generation had quite lost the linear habit—turned out not to explain much. A great piece, whatever its length, seems short, a dull piece, long. Some riveting and important pieces, cut too radically, become trivial and boring. The notion that cutting means improving came partly from the advertising department, which was failing to generate pages for text in the magazine, but mainly from the new, anti-verbal folks in graphics. People in graphics believe that space, empty or filled with busy novel forms, has value, and that printed text, meant to be read, diminishes the value of that space. They seem to regard paragraphs as units, not of meaning but of type, and to think long paragraphs of words printed in a single typeface, unadorned, "look bad." They also believe that space on the page is the key to elegance, to what Mr. Liberman, of Condé Nast, used to call "noble" layouts. It is true that, when the alternative is pictorial scraps, crowded with words in various shapes, colors, and typefaces, and bled to the page's edge, empty space comes as a relief. On the whole, however, readers, at least since the days of great illuminated manuscripts, prefer just text.

The assumption that editing means cutting, and that every piece requires it, grew, at *The New Yorker,* during Mr. Gottlieb's tenure and has grown more radically ever since. Under Ms. Brown, editors actually spoke of cutting out "filets" from books and manuscripts, and publishing those, as though the process would, like some upscale butcher, offer customers only the choicest pieces. More recently, one of the top editors explained to a friend from another magazine that *New Yorker* editors, these days, were the actual writers of pieces, regarding as hard copy and even data to be rewritten, the manuscripts that came in.

Several curious results became apparent from this assumption that the first thing a written work requires is cutting. It turns out, surprisingly, that a crucial element of the integrity of *New Yorker* pieces had been their length. Some short pieces are wonderful; many long pieces are dreary. But once cutting is regarded as a value in itself, something vital is lost. Certain levels of ambition vanish from writing altogether. There is nothing to engage more than flickers of attention from real readers. And there is no longer a space, a set of expectations, even a possibility of distinguished pieces. Long pieces cut too radically are not improved. They die. The magazine, it turned out, went with them.

As widespread, and even sometimes true, as the received wisdom was that *New Yorker* pieces had been too long, the turn to cutting for its own sake was disastrous. So were the decline in checking, and the lowering, or later the absence of, standards of taste. The imposition of "graphics," in a magazine, which had always been a vehicle essentially of prose, and whose format had once been an accidental masterpiece, was almost as unfortunate. "The visual," in several forms, began radically to change the format. Even the introduction of photographs, which had great beauty and value of their own, changed certain values that had always defined the magazine. First, almost incidentally, photographs overbalanced the cartoons. When they began to appear, not independently and on their own, but as illustrations of articles, they began to overwhelm and undercut the writing, too. Prose, in *The New Yorker,* had always carried what there was to be of physical description. The encroachments of "the visual," whether as graphics or even as great photography, changed yet another defining element of the magazine.

Even book publishing, it turns out, had succumbed to preoccupation with graphics, in another, by no means unrelated sense. The last word in books at Knopf, for example, had come to be not the author's but something like this.

> The text of this book was set in a film version of a typeface called Times Roman, designed by Stanley Morrison (1889–1967) for *The Times* (London) and first introduced by that newspaper in 1932.
>
> Among typographers and designers of the twentieth century, Stanley Morrison was a strong influence as a typographical advisor to The Monotype Corporation, as a director of two distinguished English publishing houses, and as a writer of sensibility, erudition, and keen practical sense. . . . etc.

Or even this:

> . . . In its structure Fairfield displays the sober and sane qualities of a master craftsman whose talent was long dedicated to clarity. It is this trait that accounts for the trim grace and virility, the spirited design and sensitive balance of this original type face. . . . etc.

These notes, as it happened, appeared at the end of books at Knopf. They contain information that readers, with the last line of a book still in their heads, might perhaps be willing to do without. Mr. Gottlieb, at Knopf, had been a fine editor of books. He had somehow been unable to edit *The New Yorker.* In some respects, his tenure became a blip in the history of the magazine's decline. In view of what came next, however, he was, as he had said he would be, not a radical but a conserver of the magazine.

Chapter Nine

On Thursday evening, July 9, 1992, in Newtown, Connecticut, I received another phone call, from a friend who said that tomorrow's *Wall Street Journal* would carry the news that Bob Gottlieb had been fired, and that Tina Brown had been appointed editor of the magazine. Bob Gottlieb was on vacation in Japan. I called Tina Brown at home, and got her husband, Harold Evans.

"Tina's playing with the children," he said. "Can she call you back? Can you tell me what this is about?"

"That's all right," I said. "I just called to say congratulations and best wishes."

"What for?" he asked.

"For being the new editor of *The New Yorker,*" I said.

"First I heard of it," he said; then, again, "She's playing with the children."

"That's fine," I said.

"This must be one of those silly rumors," he said. "The last one I heard was that I was being appointed editor of *The Observer,* and that she was coming to England with me."

"Well, fine," I said. "If Tina is the editor, congratulations; and if she isn't, best wishes anyway."

"What a silly idea," Mr. Evans said. "Where did you get it?"

"Well," I said. "I believe it's going to run in tomorrow's *Wall Street Journal.*" We said goodbye.

At the time of my call, it turned out, Tina and Harry were meeting with Si Newhouse. Harry immediately called *The Wall Street Journal* to tell them the story was untrue. The *Journal* killed the article—with the result that they lost their scoop. The story, based on a press release by Condé Nast, ran on Monday, July 12, simultaneously in the *Journal* and the *Times.* I had called and left a message for Bob Gottlieb. On that Monday, he returned from Japan. He called me.

"Si told me," he said, "that the magazine was everything he had hoped, but he didn't like the demographics." This, I recalled, was almost exactly what Mr. Newhouse had said to Richard Locke, when he fired him from *Vanity Fair,* and then to Leo Lerman, when he fired *him.* "Si told me that the magazine is everything he hoped," was what Mr. Lerman had said, more precisely, "but it isn't making any money." There was now a new generation, Mr. Newhouse had also said to Mr. Gottlieb, different in its tastes from Mr. Gottlieb's and his own.

"Well, I kept the magazine," Mr. Gottlieb said to me. "Perhaps improved it a little."

He spoke of "panic," at the office, at the prospect of his departure and the arrival of Tina Brown. "She's a quick study," he said. He spoke of the possibility that some people would be fired. "I'm afraid it will be the writers," he said. "You can't do without the editors." Most people expressed their sympathy, and even affection, to Mr. Gottlieb when he left. He was surprised and hurt that Mr. Gopnik dropped him without a word.

For the first months of Ms. Brown's tenure, Mr. Gottlieb continued to edit the magazine. Ms. Brown worked in separate offices, with a group she had assembled, on a strategy for revisions. Graydon Carter, who succeeded Ms. Brown at *Vanity Fair,* found himself in a difficult position. She had left him hardly any pieces. He had somehow to start from scratch, filling his magazine with whatever came to hand. In spite of a concerted and successful effort, by Ms. Brown and Condé Nast, over a period of five years, to persuade reporters from other publications that *Vanity Fair* was either in the black or about to be, the magazine had in fact been losing money on a scale unequalled since the days of a magazine published by Huntington Hartford, *Show.* It was not surprising that, in the months Mr. Carter worked to refill the well of pieces, readers thought they detected a drop in quality.

Ms. Brown's first issue of *The New Yorker* had, as its cover, a painting of a horse-drawn carriage, in New York, with a punk as its passenger. It was not as distinctly ugly as some covers under Mr. Gottlieb, and not nearly as pointlessly repellent as some of the covers that were to come. It was a statement nonetheless.

Under Tina Brown, and Steven Florio, *The New Yorker* now began to claim, excitedly, but at the same time routinely, that ads were up, subscriptions were up, newsstand sales were up, and the magazine was becoming a financial success. The magazine began to lose money on a scale that rivalled the worst days at *Vanity Fair.* The word was that Ms. Brown was sparing no expense to pay exorbitant rates to writers. The cartoonists were told they would have to wait. They would have to earn their livings elsewhere, in advertising perhaps, until the magazine turned the corner—which Ms. Brown always said it was about to do—into profitability. Writers, however, do not cost money on the scale in question. Cartoonists, even if they had been paid a living wage, would not cost money, either. What cost money was chasing readers, with by-mail solicitations, endless, costly campaigns to get them to subscribe; starting and staffing bureaus in other cities; delivering rough copies, by limousine, to people, all over the city and the world who were regarded as buzz disseminators; creating constant parties and conferences, and hiring a staff to organize them. Ms. Brown brought, from *Vanity Fair,* in a position with no previous counterpart at *The New Yorker:* her own version of a second man, at an annual salary of four hundred thousand dollars. Most expensive of all was tearing issues apart at the last minute—incurring huge costs for meaningless changes, in the name of catching trends. Most damaging, however, in both the long run and the short, was alienating readers. The financial treasure of the magazine had always been its renewal rate. Before Condé Nast began to tinker with the format, *The New Yorker* had the highest renewal rate in the history of publishing. When the format changed, and the magazine began to chase subscribers, those loyal readers who had always, almost automatically, renewed began to reconsider. When Ms. Brown began radically to change the content, the renewal rate sank like a stone.

Ms. Brown did make some changes that were for the better. She hired Bill Buford, from *Granta,* as fiction editor. She brought in pieces by Simon Schama. She discovered talent in a few young writers. She had a gift, apparently, for talking people through their stories. But in its determination to be talked about, the magazine lost its character. There was no longer anything special about it or even characteristic of it. It became a magazine like any other, only less clearly defined. There were pieces appropriate to *The New York Times Magazine, New York, Hustler.* The buzz was that the magazine was lively. What energy it had seemed to consist in irritating readers, who left in droves, to be replaced by other readers, with short attention spans, who left in turn. The buzz was also that in every issue, there was at least one piece worth reading. There was almost never any piece worth reading. *The New Yorker* and its editor were mentioned a lot in gossip columns. Ms. Brown submitted work for prizes, something no editor before Bob Gottlieb had done. The pieces, such as they were, did win awards and prizes. The magazine became, increasingly, a public relations machine for Steven Florio and Tina Brown.

Among Ms. Brown's best qualities was a considerable vitality. Even her admirers would not have claimed for her a sense of humor. Lillian Ross writes that Ms. Brown "possessed—under the usual disguises—her own share" of Mr. Shawn's "naivety, insight, and sensitivity," and, "what's more, her own hunger for wit and humor." The "usual disguises" were remarkably effective. Ms. Ross also writes that "under Tina Brown's leadership," the magazine's "losses declined dramatically." This device, not infrequent in Ms. Ross's book, is the confidently contra-factual declaration. Christopher Buckley did occasionally publish funny pieces in the magazine, but all his pieces, anywhere, were funny. Otherwise, things were bleak. The magazine kept publishing pieces by Steve Martin, Bruce McCall. With few exceptions, funny cartoons were gone. The exceptions were eclipsed by floods of material utterly subversive to the comic mood: efforts, presented as funny, that are not. Ms. Brown hired the artist Art Spiegelman, author of *Maus*, whose talent lay in cartoon narratives. His strength, it turned out, was emphatically not in painting covers. Ms. Brown then hired, as cover editor, another position that had not previously existed, Mr. Spiegelman's wife, Françoise Mouly. The covers became consistently, flatly ugly. The notion that you cannot judge a book by its cover was always metaphorical, applied literally only to books. Almost all magazines, including *The New Yorker,* had always sold at newsstands precisely on the basis of their covers. For news and fashion magazines, covers determine newsstand sales. The intention of the new covers, in so far as there was one, and of the magazine itself, evidently was to shock. The difficulty, one difficulty anyway, with this intention is that readers who are shocked tend to depart. The readers who remain are insensible to shock.

Ms. Brown did want scoops. Sometimes she got them. Sometimes they were accurate, sometimes not. There was no way *The New Yorker* could establish an identity as a serious news magazine. There were indications that she was, in fact, competing with *Vanity Fair*—which, as it happened, had begun to thrive under Graydon Carter. Once Ms. Brown engaged *Vanity Fair* on the turf of celebrity journalism, it was clear not only that *The New Yorker* could not successfully compete there, but that *Vanity Fair* had also become much the better of the two magazines. Ms. Brown's adviser on matters intellectual, whom she eventually promoted to her deputy, was a young editor named Henry Finder. Her protégé, her star in writing think-pieces, was Adam Gopnik. His work appeared often. He became the magazine's Paris correspondent, succeeding Genêt and Jane Kramer, but he addressed subjects of all kinds.

There was a characteristic structure, it turned out, to a piece by Mr. Gopnik. It began, typically, with a flourish. (1)

This is what everyone has always thought, on this topic, until this very moment. (2) What everyone has always thought, until this very moment, is incorrect. (3) Here is what I have discovered is, in fact, the case—and present to you here, at this very moment, for the first time, ever.

The real possibilities, of course, were these. (1) This was not what everybody thought, or what anybody thought, and the benighted fool under attack is a straw man. (2) This really is what everybody thought, and what everybody thought was actually right—so that either (a) Mr. Gopnik himself is quite wrong about it, or (b) his position is, in fact, in spite of its contrarian flourish, identical with what everybody thought. Or (3) What everybody thought is actually not right, and what Mr. Gopnik thinks is transparently not right either. And (4) What everybody thought was not quite right, but someone has already pointed this out—and Mr. Gopnik's position is really the position, which Mr. Gopnik either does not know or does not choose to acknowledge, of somebody else.

There were some variations, but that was the structure. Other writers have used it. The reason genuine essayists never use it is not just its built-in applause and self-congratulation. It insults the reader. This is what you thought, poor fool, along with that herd of like-minded fools to which you belonged until this minute, when you began to read this piece. No editor with any feeling for civil discourse will publish an argument that rests upon this structure. Once, perhaps. Mistakes will happen. Certainly not with any regularity.

I have come to think that fate may be as much an element of personality as any other. A person may carry with him, may *be,* his looks, his biological makeup, intelligence, disposition, education, talent, conscience, tastes, manners, even his fate. I mean something other than just his luck, good or ill, but rather a pattern—in the sort of things that happen to him. Many scientists believe that we send, and respond to, signals to and from one another, for which we have as yet no name, and of which we may not be entirely aware. Children, especially, seem to have these somewhat unaccountable transmitters and receptors. Some analogous element of our individuality may be our fate. Not immutable, certainly—just as our health and our looks are not. They are affected by events and accidents that come our way. But set, in the form of a predisposition to these events and accidents. "The boiler in the house she rented blew up," we say. "It's the sort of thing that happens to her."

The fate of *The New Yorker,* it seems, was to be, in almost every way, the contradiction of what it was designed to be and had been, against all odds, for many decades. The place that had declined to publish books, or even to permit ad hoc anthologies by Xerox, in order not to be distracted from its essence as a magazine, was suddenly, under Ms. Brown, sponsoring conferences about the future, at Disney World. These conferences, called Next, brought in, for example, an Imagineer from Disney who said from the podium, seconded by a man from Microsoft, "Let's face it. Print has only existed for five hundred years." This was, historically, not quite correct. His point, however, was not about history. Reading, he said, was coming to an end. Not an original view, perhaps, nor quite persuasive. But antithetical, certainly, to anything *The New Yorker* had been or could ever be.

The place that, rightly or wrongly, had always declined awards of every sort—Mr. Shawn himself once declined, in a single month, honorary doctorates from Harvard and from Yale—was now intriguing and plotting to get prizes. The magazine for which Senator Daniel Patrick Moynihan, in the past, an important writer for the magazine, and surely the most distinguished living senator, had achieved, on the grounds of literary value, an exemption from a rise in postal rates, had become, in many respects, a public relations firm, generating buzz about itself and its editors, in hopes of generating advertisers—a redundant and circular mechanism, in other words, for generating ads for ads, and gossip about gossip. None of these breaks with the magazine's tradition, it might be said, slowed the financial disintegration of the magazine. There were even beginning to occur problems within the gossip and the public relations campaign itself. Mr. Florio, a piece in *Fortune* revealed, had been less than candid, about his personal history and the *New Yorker*'s finances. He had always spoken of his exploits in the military. He had never served. The *Fortune* piece, and a subsequent piece in *The Wall Street Journal* even called into question what the buzz machine had always managed, in every other publication, to assert as fact: the profitability of Condé Nast.

There are, still, publications that people rush to read, on account of their regular contributors. For laughing-out-loud pieces, Dave Barry, in *The Daily News;* until recently, Russell Baker, in *The New York Times;* Mary Ann Madden's Competitions, oddly enough, in *New York* magazine. They may rush to read *Doonesbury, Boondocks,* even, still, *Peanuts.* They may rush home to read gossip columnists Liz Smith, Suzy, Cindy Adams. There is no longer anything to rush home consistently to read in *The New Yorker.* If a magazine is a person, *Vanity Fair* is Graydon Carter; *The New York Review* is Robert Silvers, and also Barbara Epstein; the *Los Angeles Times Book Review* is Steve Wasserman. *The New Yorker,* since Mr. Shawn, has been no one. If you are merely in competition with other publications for the same writers, about the same subjects, for the same audience, you may be useful, but you cannot create or sustain an important magazine. Without a tradition, or in abandoning a tradition, it is hard to see in what sense yours is a magazine at all. And in such a competition, the magazine, which was never *about* anything—as *Vogue* magazine, say, is about fashion, celebrity journalism is about gossip, and the newsmagazines are about the world in a certain week—could never win.

Some critics have suggested that Condé Nast bought *The New Yorker* largely in reaction to the embarrassment of the early issues of *Vanity Fair*, and that a failure of *The New Yorker* would be the strongest possible evidence for the notion of the graphics people, and the Disney Imagineer, and the man from Microsoft at the Next convention: that this generation simply no longer reads. Only people who don't read, and never did read, say that. It is just a cover and an excuse and a blaming of the audience, which is gone until something draws and creates it again.

Well, what was it ever, culturally, anthropologically, as a business matter, as a matter of art? It was never Camelot, or a community, or even particularly collegial. It was never a completely brilliant enterprise. There was no Balanchine here and no Lincoln Kirstein; there are no convincing disseminators of the legend. Mr. Shawn had his faults and weaknesses—a few bizarre prejudices against certain writers, whom he never published; a reluctance to overbalance his magazine, even with talent; so great a devotion to the institution that he seemed actually to resist and to limit the thriving of any particular artist, putting the ship, that is, before the passengers or even the destination. It had to sail, after all, on another day. If his dislike of confrontation extended not just to rejecting pieces but to controlling his bullies and bureaucrats, his civility left the magazine when he left it. If he had no talent for meetings or administration, he was incomparable one by one. If he had a kind of moral vanity, he had a genuine moral sense as well. It was Hannah Arendt, who wrote of Quixotic fools engaged in self-aggrandizing public performances, as opposed to "the calm good conscience of some limited achievement."

What the magazine was becomes clearer only in its absence. It used, for good or ill, to mean something to have a piece appear in *The New Yorker,* and to read it there. A succession of editorial decisions managed first to reduce, then to obliterate and actually reverse any cachet once attached to writing for it, or any particular identity attached to reading it. The priority placed on advertising and public relations over editorial content, the interference of graphics with prose, the reflexive and mindless cutting, the preoccupation with what some hypothetical readership might want, the lowering of standards of every kind—checking, taste, conscience, level of intelligence and care—did not simply waste the assets, moral, professional, cultural, financial, of the magazine itself. There was, and this is by no means unimportant, the effect of this loss on the standards of all of publishing. A magazine is not just a container. When it is alive, it creates an important community within the larger community, which is everyone. The mindless waste, of talent, good name, trust, even that invaluable subscriber base and its renewals, is just an element of what is actually gone.

As I write, the magazine will presumably be sold, or merged, or limited to occasional issues on specific themes, or simply closed. There were, in recent months, three, perhaps penultimate, instances of the ironic echo and the cackling aftermath. In the first issue under David Remnick, Ms. Brown's successor, all of Talk of the Town which had been devoted, by tradition, to a single subject only on matters of state or principle, was devoted to a sort of Festschrift for Tina Brown—making her, over a period of more than fifty years, by far the person most frequently mentioned in that section of the magazine. Charles McGrath, the editor of the *New York Times Book Review* and once a candidate for Mr. Shawn's successor, thought it proper to review Ms. Ross's book, *Here But Not Here,* in the *Times Book Review.* And *The New Yorker* itself published a review of *At Home in the World,* a memoir by Joyce Maynard. The memoir included an account of an affair between Ms. Maynard and J. D. Salinger, when Ms. Maynard was nineteen. *Vanity Fair* had excerpted a chapter—omitting accounts of sexual acts of any kind. By contrast, *The New Yorker,* in what was only a book review after all, included explicit sexual anecdotes. The ironic echo and the cackling aftermath seemed to have come full circle: a graceless and utterly unnecessary intrusion upon the privacy of one of its own, most intensely private writers, J. D. Salinger.

In my first years at *The New Yorker,* two friends wrote pieces about life as a Playboy bunny. One was Jane Kramer, who wrote her piece for *The Village Voice.* (I remember a conversation in which Jane described sitting, on a subway, near a passenger who was reading one of her pieces. He laughed throughout. When he finished, he leafed back to the beginning and read it again, laughing throughout. In the same week, I had sat, on the train, behind a passenger who read *The New Yorker* very carefully, page by page, until he got to my piece. He quickly rifled past it, and resumed reading page by page.) The other was Gloria Steinem.

Ms. Steinem has become one of the women I most admire. At that time, she was writing something called *The Beach Book,* a coffee table book, with suggestions, reasonably enough, for games to play on the beach. One day, in the course of an interview for *Glamour,* Ms. Steinem asked me how I envisioned my old age. I said I couldn't imagine it, actually, but I knew what I hoped. I hoped I would be sitting in a rocking chair beside another oldster, and agreeing with him that, in spite of what might have seemed, at the time, to be mistakes, everything had turned out to be fine. Ms. Steinem was surprised. She had never been able to imagine herself in old age otherwise than alone. I remember as well believing, and consistently saying to friends who were about to resign from this job or that, that they should not underestimate the advantages of belonging to an institution—that the world would look quite different to them, and they to the world, on their own.

Ms. Steinem's prediction turned out, in some ways, to be true for me as well. Not for me alone, however, but for a whole section of the culture. You want to have company, a person, an affiliation, a community, even in what you choose to read. Books are different. They are read alone. But magazines are communal. A beloved, complicated institution was, I think, for many reasons, lost. It is quite gone. Perhaps, in a few years, there will be another. The odds that there will be are not great, but we cannot really know.